Few understand the demonic and as a result they deal with problems their whole life that are unnecessary! Be *free!* Help others to be *free!* Simple. Profound. Life-changing!

SID ROTH
Host, *It's Supernatural!*

SECRETS TO

DESTROYING
DEMONIC
ASSIGNMENTS

SECRETS TO

DESTROYING

DEMONIC

ASSIGNMENTS

*THE ULTIMATE SPIRITUAL
WARFARE AND DELIVERANCE
HANDBOOK*

JOSHUA T. GILES

DESTINY IMAGE® PUBLISHERS, INC.

P.O. Box 310, Shippensburg, PA 17257-0310

"Promoting Inspired Lives."

This book and all other Destiny Image and Destiny Image Fiction books are available at Christian bookstores and distributors worldwide.

For more information on foreign distributors, call 717-532-3040.

Reach us on the Internet: www.destinyimage.com.

ISBN 13 TP: 978-0-7684-6428-3

ISBN 13 eBook: 978-0-7684-6429-0

ISBN 13 HC: 978-0-7684-6431-3

ISBN 13 LP: 978-0-7684-6430-6

For Worldwide Distribution, Printed in the U.S.A.

2 3 4 5 6 7 8 / 27 26 25 24 23

CONTENTS

INTRODUCTION

Let me tell you a bit about one of my first supernatural encounters with God. I was taken in the spirit—this was not a dream or a vision. My spirit man literally left my body. It is like your body and soul/spirit man are held together with Velcro. God reached down to me and pulled my spirit man out of my body. He took me out to show me things that were actually happening in the spirit world, behind the scenes. It was completely different from having a vision or dream in the spirit. In the book of Revelation, John wrote, *"I was caught up in spirit on the Lord's day"* and he saw all these happenings in the spirit world (Revelation

1:10 NABRE). This has occurred many times in Scripture to different individuals.

In my experience, the Lord reached down and put His hand upon my neck and took me in the spirit. It's impossible to describe this experience other than it reveals what reality actually is in the spirit world. You may experience super intense dreams, but this kind of experience is totally different and on another level. It is like the contrast between watching a black and white TV compared to super-HDTV. It is honestly mind-blowing. Being taken in the spirit is another level of intensity.

When I encountered God this way, I saw God face to face in the spirit. I touched His eye. I wrote more in-depth about this in my other book. But after this spiritual encounter, I was able to bring it into the natural to function in the glory and in the anointing. Sometimes, God will take His servants in the spirit to show them the reality going on behind the scenes. This isn't something that happens every day. This is not a common occurrence. These supernatural encounters are few and far between. Personally, I have had these experiences about 20 times in my life at this level of encounter. I have been on this spiritual journey with God for about 15 years and will have a supernatural encounter of this magnitude about one and a half to two times a year, every year. When this occurs, it is super intense.

The first time I was taken in the spirit, the hand of the Lord came upon me, just like the prophet was taken. This is when I had just started in ministry. The Lord came upon me. His hand was bigger than my body. It was very wild! I had just come home from attending a Baptist church. I was going to a Baptist church, but I prayed in tongues and I was just learning all these things in the spirit. I really didn't know what was going on. I was literally brand-new, learning about the supernatural in this way. I came home and was extremely tired and felt that I just needed to lie down. This extreme exhaustion came upon me—a very unusual tiredness I've never experienced before. As I went to lie down, the hand of God came upon me and snatched me out of my body. I was blown away at the reality of how small I was compared to the actual hand of God. In reality, we as humans are just tiny puppets. God took me to a family member's house and dropped me there. I sat in a fighter stance. When you are in the spirit like this, you feel so different and move and operate so differently. You travel at the speed of light.

I was in the spirit at this house; and the walls and the structure of the house were there, but I could also see through those physical restrictions. I could see through the physical walls, so I knew that there was a witch in the back room. I said, "What are you doing here?"

The witch said to me, "You know why I'm here."

The moment that we had that conversation, exactly at that moment, the fire and power of God left me. Then God's hand was back in the room, bigger than my body, pushing me to engage that witch. I was thinking, *You're pushing me into a battle and I'm going to die.* I knew I was not ready. I said in my heart, "Do you not see that the fire and the power have left me?" It was like God didn't care—He was pushing me to engage that witch.

As He pushed me, I knew a doorway was around the corner, and the witch was there in that back room. So I put my hands against the wall and I fought, trying to slow down the forward motion toward that room. I was screaming like a little child, "No, no, no, I don't want to do it! I don't want to do it! I don't want to do it!" Right when I got to the corner where the battle would occur with the witch, God snatched me up and took me back and dropped me in my body.

I jumped up from that experience thinking, *What in the world?* I did not know what had happened, but I knew it was real and it was by the Spirit of God that I had this encounter. I know when God begins to move and bring freedom to His people. I see Him bringing freedom to your mind and freedom from fear. Fear is being removed and has no place in your life. The purpose of this testimony is to strengthen your faith and eliminate fear. It is to bring liberation from the chains of fear.

When I got back to my body from that supernatural encounter, I realized that this was not like anything I had ever experienced before. I did not know of anyone who had ever had this type of encounter, and I couldn't share it with anyone for years. Many years later, I received the revelation that when you are seeking God, He will take you through supernatural encounters. Those spiritual experiences will teach you so much that you will still be learning from that revelation and experience for years to come.

You may say to yourself, "Is this normal?" Let me frame this for you to have a deeper understanding of spiritual warfare. We all have been empowered by the Holy Spirit to walk out a victorious life over the enemy. Every believer, from a beginner to a veteran, will experience demonic attack, but learning how to respond and how to interpret the encounter will make the difference.

I want to help you understand that no matter what I tell you, nothing is ever to make you feel afraid. As your identity in Christ starts to develop and boldness arises within you, you will learn that no matter what the enemy brings you will never feel timid. The Bible says the righteous are as bold as a lion and the wicked flee when no one pursues them. We should all continue to pursue God knowing that no matter what the enemy throws our way, we are victorious. We just have to know how to engage the enemy in order to see the results that are promised in God's Word. Through this book you will be empowered beyond anything you could imagine when it comes to destroying demonic assignments. There is absolutely nothing to fear!

CHAPTER 1

ENGAGE AND DESTROY

E ngage and destroy. This is one of the things that God taught me many years ago when the Holy Spirit began to train me. *Engage and destroy* to understand the very aspect of spiritual warfare I was always intrigued by. What is the proper way to engage? What do we do when we are trying to really understand two key questions of spiritual warfare? Number one, how is the enemy functioning? Number two, how do we win battles? I remember clearly one night I had a supernatural experience where God began to explain this in-depth. He said, "Let me teach you something, because most people are afraid to engage the enemy. Most people are afraid to have spiritual encounters. The reason they are afraid is because what happens in the spiritual realm is so much more real than the natural realm. When someone gets a taste of what's happening behind the scenes in the Spirit, if they are not fully prepared in understanding who they are in Christ and where they stand in authority, they will constantly lose because fear will engulf them."

The church has been conditioned to fear through entertainment, through social media, through different atmospheres, and through environments. Fear is the ruling force that causes people in the body of Christ to lose spiritual battles. When most people have a terrifying dream or vision, their response is full of fear. They wake up and say, "Oh my gosh, that was so crazy!" Their experience is so terrifying, but their response to it is the key. To respond in fear is not the proper way to win the battle. Many supernatural encounters occur in the middle of the night mainly because we are vulnerable in our sleep. When you fall asleep, you are in a much deeper state to perceive the things that are happening in the spirit realm.

For those who have a greater level of perception, their experiences are amplified. People who are gifted in the prophetic experience an amplified dream life or vision life. Because of this reality, if they are not properly trained to execute God's game plan in warfare, they will lose every battle. This is particularly dangerous to those who have a prophetic gifting because they tend to be very sensitive to the things of the spirit. If they do not understand how to wage a good warfare and if they are ignorant of the principles of engagement in the spirit realm, they have the potential to bring harm and confusion to the body of Christ. An unseasoned prophetic person can unknowingly receive wrong interpretations and experience visitations by demonic forces dressed as the angel of light. Because they do not have the proper training, understanding, and discerning of spirits, they misinterpret these encounters as God encounters when in reality it is satan masquerading as light.

God is a good God who is gracious to us. He prepares us to fight these spiritual battles in the same way that David was prepared in the sheep pasture. David was prepared to face Goliath because he first encountered and killed the lion and the bear on the back side of the wilderness. In the same way, we aren't left alone without instruction or insight on how to engage and interact with the supernatural. God gives us the blueprint to victory and living an overcoming life.

Under the first covenant, we read of physical warfare taking place. Armies were defeated. Intense battles were the norm. Unusual supernatural things occurred like the prophets calling down actual fire from heaven or defeating the enemy by putting the praise team on the front lines of the battlefield. God gave the children of Israel detailed instructions in the Old Testament that were specific to that time and season.

After Jesus completed His assignment on earth, the way believers engaged with God and the supernatural drastically changed. He is the way to the Father and to an increased revelation of the things of the spirit. The New Testament emphasizes the battle of the spirit, not the flesh. In 1 Corinthians, Paul explains that under this new covenant, we don't wrestle against flesh and blood but against principalities, rulers of darkness, and spiritual wickedness in high places. If we never come to the full understanding of how to operate in the spirit realm, how to dismantle what is happening behind the scenes, it is impossible to live a truly victorious life in the natural. This is why so many Christians live in a beat-down mentality. There are so many believers who are gifted in the spirit but they lose battle after battle, because they truly have not grasped the understanding of what it takes to be victorious through spiritual warfare.

The problem with the Western church in this day and age is that there is too much fluff-cake Christianity. They want to sing and dance you happy and tickle your ears with messages and entertainment that does nothing to provoke you to holiness. There is no emphasis on walking in the anointing that you were designed to carry or to bearing up the cross it takes to do so. Most people just want constant encouragement and never truly want to go through the process of discipleship. This has caused many Christians to become casualties of war. This type of mentality runs through the majority of the Western church.

TRAINING GROUNDS

As I began to learn through multiple supernatural encounters spanning over seven hundred days of consistent warfare engagement, God was using these experiences to teach me how to be victorious. My teacher was not man—it was the

Holy Spirit in these moments. As I faced these encounters with the demonic and principalities, I knew these moments of reality in the spirit realm were where everything happens. We are not recognized by natural titles or whatever we think we carry in the natural; we are recognized by what mantle and what anointing we truly possess in the spirit. The enemy only recognizes that level of authority.

We see this in the Scriptures with the story of the seven sons of Sceva in Acts. They saw the mighty works of Paul and how evil spirits responded and left people when he used the name of Jesus.

> *Then some of the itinerant Jewish exorcists undertook to invoke the name of the Lord Jesus over those who had evil spirits, saying, "I adjure you by the Jesus whom Paul proclaims." Seven sons of a Jewish high priest named Sceva were doing this. But the evil spirit answered them, "Jesus I know, and Paul I recognize, but who are you?" And the man in whom was the evil spirit leaped on them, mastered all of them and overpowered them, so that they fled out of that house naked and wounded* (Acts 19:13-16 ESV).

We can catch a revelation here and see that true authority was recognized in the spirit realm. When Jesus walked the earth, unknown in the natural to anyone as the anointed Messiah, demons trembled in terror because they understood that He was different from other men. "Jesus I know" means there was an immediate recognition that this Man was completely different than any other man they had seen. Then the Scripture goes on to say, "Jesus I know, and Paul I recognize." When the spirit said, "Paul I recognize," it knew that although this man might have similar weaknesses as other men, he also carried a different type of authority than other men. This is why the spirit said, "I recognize this one."

Paul had come under the ambassadorship of Christ as a recognized official of the kingdom of God in full authority and fully aware of who Jesus is. There is no respecter of persons with God. But because of pride in the church, many people are claiming authority and mantles they do not possess. True power is demonstrated when what you say comes to pass. If I want to see the evidence of God's power and backing in your life, I must see that the words of your mouth and your actions carry a response in the natural realm. There must be a supernatural component to your life that is extremely recognizable even to the secular world.

SPIRITUAL AUTHORITY

So what does *engage and destroy* mean? When God began to teach me this terminology, it was something that would be carried through over a lifetime of encounters. Engage and destroy is a mentality that must be taken into the spirit realm whenever something takes place. It is something that will be so embedded into you that it becomes second nature. When God began to train me in spiritual battles, He didn't throw me into principalities at first. There are not many people who are ready to engage the supernatural at that level; principalities do not recognize just any believer. We can see examples throughout history of what it means to have kingdom authority. An emperor or king will decree a thing in a kingdom and it is established. Their authority precedes them. They can also delegate some of that authority through royal symbols, such as their cloak or signet ring. This is a symbol to other people in that kingdom that the bearer now has the same authority as the king or is operating with direct orders from the ruler or king. When I started seeing spiritual rulers of regions and cities, I knew that God had called me to a specific mantle of authority.

The first battles that I started undergoing were literally demons visiting me. At first, I was terrified. I didn't know how to respond. I would wake up from an encounter and begin to pray to God. I wondered why I felt strong and powerful in the natural as I prayed and pursued God, but when I began to encounter the demonic a level of fear and insecurity overcame me. The Holy Spirit began to speak to me and say that I really didn't know who I was in Christ. I needed to pursue my rightful standing as someone with authority in the realm of the spirit, and only then would I be able to overcome any encounter that I experienced in the realm of the spirit. That didn't make too much sense to me at first. In my mind, I thought I knew who I was and what God had called me to do, but in reality I had not carved out enough pursuit in the Lord. I had not dedicated time to prayer and fasting to really have that characteristic or attribute downloaded into my spirit man.

When these supernatural encounters occurred, I responded based on my instinct because it was interwoven into my very being. This is why it is imperative that we constantly pursue God. When we pursue Him, He begins to develop disciplines within us. We grow in maturity and understanding when it comes to our identity. Misplaced or unknown identity is the number-one problem, not only in Christianity but in the world. Most people have no clue who they are! We have to understand that identity is not just acquired at the door of salvation. Identity is found in our continual pursuit. As we begin to pursue God through the Scriptures about how He sees us, only then can our identity be revealed. Only then can our character be shaped to see ourselves as He sees us.

Jeremiah 29:11 (NIV) says, "*For I know the plans I have for you,' declares the Lord, 'plans to prosper you and not to harm you, plans to give you hope and a future.'*" We can see here God has plans for our life, but unfortunately many believers never can see from this standpoint. They only see the natural circumstances or surroundings speaking to their life. They cannot see that God has a hope-filled future and many desires for them. As I began to read Jeremiah 29:11, I began to meditate on the Word of God. Joshua 1:8 instructs us to meditate on the book of the law day and night and whatever we do, we shall find success.

As I began to meditate upon the truth that God wants to prosper me and not harm me and that He has plans for me, I began to formulate my process of seeking Him. My prayer life and fasting began to shift my perception and understanding of my identity in Christ. Many people in the church are suffering an identity crisis. They start to formulate their identity based solely on prophetic words, encouragement, and the thoughts and opinions of others. This will always lead to an incorrect perception of self. They begin to take in negativity from others and view themselves in the light of those words. Maybe they have experienced emotional pain or church hurt and now that is where they find their identity. Allowing your identity to be shaped by outside variables will always result in the wrong identity. You are not what happened to you or what you have done. Jesus paid the price for every soul to find their true identity as a child of God, no matter the circumstance or situation. Your identity should be shaped by the Word of God. Only when you begin to meditate upon the Word of God, when you begin to pray upon it and fast in pursuit of God, can He begin to develop your inner man to see as He sees and hear what He declares over you.

As I received this revelation, God began to take me into more encounters of testing with the demonic. In those moments, I began to see victory as I allowed the boldness of who I knew I was and the authority I carried to destroy the assignment of the enemy. The moment you come to a place of knowing who you are in Christ and begin to exercise the authority that you have been given in the spirit, the enemy becomes terrified of you! You will begin to be recognized in the spirit, just like the demons recognized Paul in the encounter with the sons of Sceva. This is the meaning of *engage and destroy*.

The Lord Is on Your Side

I remember when God began to teach me. In the moments when I would go into a supernatural encounter and fear would start to grip me, I would always lose. This type of supernatural encounter is not a dream or a vision. Dreams and visions are a portion and glimpse into what is happening in the spirit. I was literally taken into the realm of the spirit. Being taken into the realm of the spirit is the deepest level of experience you can have as a human because you are literally in the spiritual realm where everything exists. God actually takes your spirit man out of your body. There are examples all throughout Scripture. One example is found in Acts 8. An angel of the Lord spoke to Philip and told him to travel down from Jerusalem to Gaza, which was a desert. As he journeyed on his way, an Ethiopian eunuch passed him on the road to Jerusalem. He was sitting in his chariot, reading Isaiah the prophet. The Holy Spirit instructed Philip to approach the Ethiopian and explain the Scriptures that he was reading and preach Jesus to him. The Ethiopian received Christ and was baptized right there, but as he came up from the water Philip was caught up by the Spirit of the Lord and was found at Azotus. He was literally taken up in the spirit to another physical location (see Acts 8:26-40).

The first time I had this type of experience, as I explained in the Introduction, the hand of the Lord came upon me and pulled me up like there was Velcro on the back of my neck. I vividly remember detaching from my body and traveling to an unknown place, which turned out to be my home. The moment I was dropped into that geographical location, the fire of the Holy Spirit was burning over me from head to toe. I have never experienced anything like that in my life to that level. I knew that there was a witch in a room down the hallway. Immediately, I cried out, "What are you doing here?"

She said, "You know why I'm here."

The moment I heard those words, fear gripped my heart and I lost the fire. Literally, the fire was completely extinguished. The moment this happened, the hand of God, which was larger than the size of my body, began to push me down the hallway to engage this witch. I was clawing, scratching, and screaming, "No, no, no, I don't want to!" The moment I turned the corner where the engagement was going to happen, God snatched me back up by my neck and placed me back in my body. I had never experienced anything like that in my life.

Years of revelation came from that powerful moment. It's amazing to me to know that it only takes an inkling of fear to cause you to lose battles in the spirit. It is truly mind-blowing to me that it only took just a little bit of fear entering my heart and mind and instantly the fire of the Holy Spirit was gone. What does this teach us? We must know who we are in Christ! Our identity as a believer and the authority that we possess must be engraved within us. This was one of the most important lessons God has ever taught me. From that moment forward, I began to experience more situations like this. This led up to my face-to-face encounter with the living God, which is detailed in my book *Secrets to an Encounter with God*. What I experienced was so terrifying that if I focused on it, I believe I would have lost the experience altogether. My first book recounts that experience and how that encounter brought me to a place where I touched the eye of God.

Over the years, as God began to teach me spiritual warfare through these encounters, the words kept coming back to me—engage and destroy. As I began to pray into this revelation, I realized that I must be the one who engages the enemy. No hesitation, no thought process, but just pure reaction to engage and destroy, like a lion attacking whatever is in front of me. I was actually so excited after receiving this revelation that I looked forward to demons visiting me. The Bible says in Proverbs 28:1 (ESV), *"The wicked flee when no one pursues, but the righteous are bold as a lion."* We must take that stance! We should have ferocity and boldness and take that craziness in the realm of the spirit! Satan only recognizes spiritual violence. He operates in that realm. But *"the kingdom of heaven suffers violence, and the violent take it by force"* (Matthew 11:12 NKJV). Sugar-coated, fluff-cake Christianity will get you destroyed in the realm of the spirit. This is why the majority of believers never truly have supernatural encounters. It is God's mercy because they would not survive.

As I applied this instruction to engage the enemy no matter what stood before me, God began to show me principalities and millions of demons in the spirit. Without hesitation, no matter what atmosphere of fear or delusion satan tried to throw at me, I would run full force at the enemy. This strategy shifted everything. I began to win every battle in the spirit. The majority of the time, the enemy was so terrified I didn't even have to engage him. The process of pursuing him terrified him. Most Christians do not respond this way in battle, and that is why the enemy has the upper hand. From this moment forward, you now have the revelation of how to win every battle in the spirit!

DECLARATIONS

I RENOUNCE EVERY CLAIM OF FEAR
ON MY LIFE IN THE NAME OF JESUS.

I RENOUNCE EVERY COVENANT I HAVE
MADE WITH FEAR, UNKNOWINGLY OR
KNOWINGLY, IN THE NAME OF JESUS.

I AM AS BOLD AS A LION, IN JESUS' NAME.

I SEEK YOUR KINGDOM AND I SEEK YOUR
RIGHTEOUSNESS, IN THE NAME OF JESUS.

I DESTROY EVERY ATMOSPHERE OF DELUSION
AND DECEPTION THAT SATAN IS USING TO TRY
TO CAUSE ME TO FEAR, IN THE NAME OF JESUS.

I DECREE CONFIDENCE IN WORD, IN
SPEECH, AND IN ACTION, IN JESUS' NAME.

I DECREE THAT I WILL NEVER FEAR
WHENEVER I AM FACING A BATTLE IN
THE SPIRIT, IN THE NAME OF JESUS.

HOLY SPIRIT, TEACH ME HOW TO ENGAGE
AND DESTROY, IN THE NAME OF JESUS.

Prayer of Activation

Father, I pray in the mighty name of Jesus that every person reading these words will experience supernatural victories. I declare that the very foundations of the enemy will begin to shake and crumble in their life, in Jesus' mighty name. I declare that every spirit of fear is uprooted out of their foundation, in Jesus' mighty name. Every lie, every deception, and every delusion of the enemy attempting to make them think that God is not bigger than the situation or the problem they face, I cast it down by fire in Jesus' name! I prophesy over every one that fear is completely eradicated from their life. I prophesy boldness and confidence in every area of their lives, in Jesus' mighty name.

CHAPTER 2

HOW TO DISCERN WITCHES AND WITCHCRAFT

Let's begin with the very definition of witchcraft according to the Bible and contrast that definition with the perspective of the secular world. Witchcraft is the practice of magic, especially black magic—the use of spells. These practices typically include sorcery or magic. Witchcraft traditionally means the use of supernatural powers to harm others or to control people or events. A practitioner of witchcraft is a witch (female) or a warlock (male). Witchcraft is classified as the communication with the devil or with a familiar spirit. Witchcraft rituals and practices that incorporate a belief in magic are associated especially with pagan religions and traditions such as Wicca. Wiccan priests and priestesses often attend interfaith meetings and are able to easily connect with people who practice Catholicism, Judaism, and Buddhism. These three religions have sects within them that actually pull some high-level witchcraft into their offshoot doctrines.

Many Wiccans will describe their faith as a revival of primitive pagan rituals, believing spiritual power comes from the sun, the moon, and the earth rather than from the God of the Bible. Many seemingly innocent items are actually used in the practice of witchcraft, including spellcasting stones and crystals. Many are sold as souvenirs to tourists. Other people unknowingly pick up items used in magic and philosophy. We will take a closer look at these types of objects later on in this book.

Witchcraft can be found in all professions and workplaces. Wiccans or people who practice witchcraft will often wear five-pointed stars called pentagrams and moon necklaces and other small signals to seek out and identity others. Anytime you see someone who is infatuated by the moon or constantly wearing clothing or jewelry associated with the moon, that person is either bound by the spirit of witchcraft unknowingly or they are actually a practicing witch. Wiccans see earth as endowed with powers and energies that humans can call upon and use for specific reasons or purposes through various rituals. In other words, this is how they cast spells. Intense meditation and concentration by individuals or the unified group is the core of spellcasting. Just as the Bible says, *"For where two or three are gathered together in My name, I am there in the midst of them"* (Matthew 18:20 NKJV), there is a specific atmosphere that is created when people come together, like-minded in agreement.

We see this with the tower of Babel. This is the only time recorded in the Bible when God came down and scattered their voices. When we look at the tower of Babel, we see that historically the building was only about 300 feet tall. When compared to today's skyscrapers, 300 hundred feet is not really that tall. How was it that they were able to get God's attention? How was it that they were able to get Him to say, "If I do not stop them, they will reach heaven"? If we look at the natural perspective, we understand that there was no way they could truly break out of the stratosphere into the solar system or outer space. That's not logical. The natural atmosphere of earth would prevent that from actually happening. They would die from no oxygen and they would freeze to death because of the temperature in outer space.

So how was it that they would have been able to reach heaven if they continued? Number one—the Bible says that they had all came together with one mind with one intention. That is the power of unity! Number two—at top of the tower were occult symbols and pentagrams by which they performed sacrifices, blood rituals, and sexual rituals. All of these are keys that allow illegal entry into the spirit realm. Certain occult symbols are literally keys that unlock atmospheres to the spirit realm. It is very common for satanic rituals, rituals performed by witches and people in the occult, to have symbolism as a very strong component to their ritual and the outcome they are seeking. Through the centuries, these specific symbols have not changed.

Blood Covenants

Another key component in these rituals is the shedding of blood. This is a very spiritual act. When Jesus shed His blood, it was an act that was done in the natural but it had impact for all of eternity because of the spiritual ramifications behind it. Although we don't physically see the blood of Jesus, as believers His blood is our representative in the spirit realm. The blood carries life force. There is life in the blood. This is where the soul dwells. When we see Cain killing his righteous brother, Abel, the Bible says that Abel's blood began to cry out from the ground. Blood is the life force. This is one reason why God gave a commandment in the Old Testament not to eat the blood of an animal because it is the life force of the animal. People who practice witchcraft and are in the occult use blood as a key to open the door to the spirit realm.

Blood rituals are probably the most powerful component when it comes to accessing the spirit realm and demons. Blood rituals and blood covenants are imperative to gaining occult power. This is why the type of blood that is used gives the witch or person practicing more enforcing power. It gives more power to the demons when doing the ritual. From animals to human sacrifice (abortion), the type of blood carries different "energies" as they label it. The mixture of symbolism and blood creates a powerful opening in the spirit realm for access.

We now see the power of communion as described in the Bible when we partake in the bread as His body and the juice/wine as His blood. The Bible says to do this continually *"in remembrance of Me"* until Christ returns (see Luke 22:19 NKJV). This is a powerful component of the Christian walk. If communion is neglected, often there is deterioration in fellowship with Christ.

The blood of Jesus was shed for us once in the natural and still carries power throughout all of eternity in the spirit realm. The shedding of His blood washed away all our sins for eternity. Shedding of blood never has to happen again for the remission of our sins. Observing communion is a powerful representation and key that Christ has set forth in the Word that gives legal access to the spirit realm. Demonic manipulation and the occult enter illegally. This is why demons control practitioners of witchcraft. They also cannot just do a blood ritual once and that's it. Blood has to constantly be shed in order to empower their rituals, spells, and demons. Believers must understand when engaging in spiritual warfare that you have the ability to cancel every demonic shedding of blood against your life, against your family, and against your region or country. Unless you are praying this type of prayer, you have a lot of demonic forces coming against you unmatched and unhindered.

Witches follow the observance of the sun and the moon. They call it "days of power." The Bible says something very powerful in the book of Psalms with David in relation to this subject. It says, *"The sun shall not strike you by day, nor the moon by night"* (Psalm 121:6 NKJV). This is a powerful statement. If we look at this from the natural standpoint, we understand that obviously the sun can burn you if you stand in it all day, but what can the moon do to you physically? The Bible was not referring to the physical effects of the sun and moon on people. This passage refers to the witchcraft that can be performed or programmed using the sun or moon as a point of contact. David understood that these rituals were part of the agenda of the enemy against God's people. When you have an understanding of what the practitioners of witchcraft operate in, you can see that God has placed in our power the ability to counteract every demonic effect against our life. I have done countless deliverances of those affected by moon witchcraft.

Prayer of Activation

> Everything that has been programmed in the sun, the moon, or the stars against my life by any witch or by any warlock, I destroy you by the fire of the Holy Ghost, in the name of Jesus.

Pharmakeia is the mixing of potions, spells, and sorcery. High-level people in the occult and witchcraft truly understand that if they are to connect with supernatural beings, they need to associate and work with psychedelic drugs that open them up to the spirit realm. This is a strong practice for those who operate at this high level of witchcraft and understand what it opens them up to. Revelation 9:21 (AMP) says, *"And they did not repent of their murders nor of their sorceries (drugs, intoxications) nor of their [sexual] immorality nor of their thefts."* Sorceries, in this context, deal with the drugs and the intoxications of witchcraft. This is so important as it is written in 1 Peter 5:8 (NKJV), *"Be sober, be vigilant; because your adversary the devil walks about like a roaring lion, seeking whom he may devour."*

Whenever we step outside of sobriety by the use of drugs, we literally engage in the spirit realm illegally. This is one-way witchcraft that can attach to you unknowingly. When people begin to dabble in drug use, they are literally opening up the door to the demonic realm. Many visitations of so-called guardian angels are actually demonic forces masquerading as guardian angels. Drug use opens the door to these types of encounters. The Bible says that satan appears as an angel of light. Psychedelic and hard drugs that create dream-like hallucinations truly open the door to this type of supernatural experience.

Witches practice individually or by gathering in groups called circles or covens. They call on the deities to guide them using specific magic. They often repeat an oath: "As long as it harms none, do what you will." The problem with this oath is that this mantra was created by one of the wickedest men to walk the earth, Alastair Crowley. Alastair Crowley created this statement, "Do as thou wilt shall be the whole of the law," which is a direct counter response against God's Word. He was one of the most high-level occult leaders in the world. He was often associated with blood sacrifice, the eating of babies, and had extreme influence even into this generation. If you were to know how many people were connected to Crowley's work, how many artists and others listened to his teachings, you would be mortified. A massive number of musicians love this man and have attributed their influence directly to his teachings.

CHAPTER 3

DIFFERENT LEVELS OF WITCHCRAFT

Rebellion is as of the sin of witchcraft. When people live in rebellion, rebellion is the dominating spirit that is affecting them. You will see this in their speech and in their actions. A blind witch is someone who doesn't even know that they are used as a puppet by the enemy. This is hard to believe, but in every church there are some blind witches in operation. They look nice, they love the Lord, they prophesy, they can even operate in the gifts of the Spirit, but because they have refused to surrender completely to the will of God, there is a root of rebellion operating within them. How much they surrender to that rebellion will dictate how strong of a witchcraft spirit functions through them.

Now let me say something here, because you need to know this. There are two types of people. There are people who refuse to listen and change, or resist counsel, or even say they're willing to change but never put forth the action. Then there are those who are steel bound by the same spirit and may be in a bad place, but they are so surrendered to the process that they are willing to do whatever it takes to be set free. This is why you see a lot of "unqualified" people operating in huge levels of freedom and in the power of the Spirit, while people who have been in the church most of their life are dead as a doornail. A prostitute can come up and surrender to Christ, and within days she can be operating in the power of the Holy Spirit simply because her level of surrender to freedom is different than the person who is in the church, thinks they know God, and believes they don't need deliverance.

I believe this is why many times in the Bible, the people Jesus was around and the ones who were anointed with power, like His disciples and Mary Magdalene the prostitute, ended up doing powerful things for the kingdom. This is an example of a problem within the church. I can't tell you how many people God has highlighted to me and called me to mentor that 99 percent of the church would cast aside. I prayed in my early years of ministry that God would give me the ability to see motives and see what God wants to do in a person, so I began to speak to what I saw in the spirit, not to what I saw in the natural.

Please understand that just because someone may be bound up under the torment of this spirit, it does not mean that they have become your enemy. You have to discern whether they truly want to be free or not. By that determination, you have your next course of action. I have seen many people who are completely afflicted and attacked and under the power of the spirit of witchcraft, because they did not understand how to get freedom. Yet if their heart is completely open to instruction, that is a completely different circumstance. As I take that person through deliverance and begin to mentor them, I see the gold that God has put within them start to come to the surface.

Now on the flip side, if someone is completely bound up with this spirit and they refuse instruction, they refuse to be helped out of their torment, or they do not put forth the action to be set free, you have to determine your level of engagement with that individual. Someone who refuses to hear your voice or listen to what it takes to be set free can be prayed for from a distance. This is not the person you bring close to you. It is very vital to discern how to help people in this situation. Pride and rebellion are a serious stench in the spirit. I get around some ministers and I am disgusted and can't even stand to be in their presence because of how much pride is seeping out from them. That type of person I would never bring correction to or even reveal things that I have seen about them, because they are not in a position to receive it. Proximity to me depends on the heart condition. People will not be close to me if their heart is not in the right position. That is the level of discernment God has given me and it's something you should seek after also. A person's relationship with God determines their access with me. I don't let many people close, and it's not that I don't choose it; it's that God chooses it.

So we understand that when someone is unknowingly under the influence of a spirit of witchcraft, the term that we use is a *blind witch*. They exhibit many different signs that show that they are under the domination and influence of this spirit. Every person who is not born again definitely deals with this spirit. Whether it is the dominant one or not, one of the root demons operating is witchcraft.

As far as those who are in the church, there is a large percentage of people who have been under the influence of this demon at many different levels of manifestation. For some, it is so minute that it is a hard thing to pick out unless you have strong discernment. Those in the church who manifest this spirit at a much stronger level usually have many different telling signs that this spirit is influencing them. You can almost always see it in what they wear, items they may have at home, specific movies, and music that they enjoy. They are usually associated with deceit or drama. These types of people have things around them that are connected to the spirit because it creates an atmosphere of empowering the spirit upon them.

For example, I have done thousands of deliverances that involved removing certain necklaces, rings, or artifacts and items around the house that had been dedicated to the enemy. These are not so easily recognized by the natural eye. That is why you must have the gift of discerning of spirits. At the battle of Ai, Joshua went up against the Philistines and lost the battle. He began to cry out and ask, "Why did we lose?" God responded, "There is an item that has been dedicated to destruction in your camp; therefore, I cannot fight for you." You see, when we bring what is dedicated to destruction into our home or place it on our bodies ignorantly, we can place ourselves in a position of losing battles consistently in the spirit.

This is why you must begin to examine yourself with everything that you have a strong desire for that's drawing you. Begin to really ask the Holy Spirit, "Am I being drawn to this because a spirit is drawing me?" When you begin to do self-examination, the Holy Spirit will begin to reveal to you everything that needs to be removed—everything that is hindering you from moving forward. When I first learned this revelation I was so shocked. This is how the process works. As you begin to renounce witchcraft and anything associated with it and you let that be your prayer, you'll begin to see the Holy Spirit reveal to you anything that is associated with that spirit. This is God's mercy to deliver you from something you didn't even know was affecting you.

There are many different levels of ranking when it comes to witches. We will take a look at these levels from a natural perspective in the secular world and also from a church perspective. The first type of witch that we will review is the blind witch. I don't want you to get confused by the terminology, because usually when people think of the word *witch* they automatically assume that this individual is knowingly and intentionally practicing spells, dark magic, etc. In reality, the first level of initiation is when the spirit of witchcraft comes upon a person or influences them unawares. This type of oppression is felt by the individual in many different ways—endless cycles of negativity in their life, bad dreams, confusion, constant drama, or what they may call "bad luck," so to speak. They usually live in a perpetual cycle of complaining and murmuring.

CLOSING DOORS TO THE DEMONIC

Let's break down how the spirit of witchcraft begins to infiltrate these individuals and initiate them without their knowledge. One of the first steps that the enemy uses is rebellion in the bloodline. All humans are born into rebellion. The Bible says, "*In sin my mother conceived me*" (Psalm 51:5 NKJV), meaning that we are all born into sin. The precious blood of Jesus redeems us from that fact, but there is always the issue of rebellion trying to rear its ugly head to call us to that place of resisting God. The Bible says that rebellion is as the sin of witchcraft. What most Christians do not understand is that there are many people in the church who are plagued by witchcraft spirits and they don't even know it simply because rebellion is the driving force in their life, even though they believe in Christ. Although they have accepted Christ, they live a defeated life because they don't realize that they have to break out of those cycles of rebellion and sin in order to live victoriously in every area of their life.

You see, just because you accept Jesus Christ and you are a Christian does not mean you do not need deliverance. In reality, when you become a born-again believer the deliverance process has just started. We must begin to fast and pray while renouncing any claim of the enemy over our life. We have to renounce rebellion and pride. We have to renounce the lusts of the flesh, the lust of the eyes, and the pride of this life. We have to renounce ungodliness and worldly desire. These are the driving force of the enemy's plan to destroy people. The world is made up of these three—the lusts of the flesh, the lust of the eyes, and the pride of this life.

The following prayer should be part of your prayer life as long as you live. This is not a prayer that you just pray and leave it alone. The enemy is constantly looking for ways to place the yoke of bondage upon your life. He uses the natural realm—your experiences, your relationships with people—or the spirit realm through your dreams and encounters. Satan is constantly trying to place yokes upon you. A yoke is a dominating force; it is a structure of slavery in the spirit. A yoked ox is driven by his master. In the same way, the enemy tries to put believers in a yoke of bondage. Sin is a yoke. But the Bible says, "*the yoke will be destroyed because of the anointing*" (Isaiah 10:27 NKJV). Unless there is an anointing associated with your walk, you will always be a defeated soldier.

This is a prayer you must memorize because in order to keep yourself on the cutting edge and your perception of the things of the spirit sharp, you must continually keep dealing with these areas. It is satan's entryway to initiate rebellion and destruction into your life. The Bible says to produce fruit in keeping with repentance (see Matthew 3:8). Now that we understand how rebellion is initiated through our lives, we will be more aware of what to deal with as we pray, fast, and seek the Lord.

Prayer of Activation

I renounce every worldly desire, every ungodliness, the lusts of the flesh, the lust of the eyes, the pride of this life, and all rebellion in the name of Jesus.

I renounce every spirit of witchcraft in the name of Jesus.

I renounce every spirit of rebellion and stubbornness operating in my bloodline, in Jesus' name.

Every stronghold of resistance to the things of God in my life, I pull you down by the mighty weapons of God, in Jesus' name.

I pull out every high place of rebellion, in the name of Jesus.

I pull down every high place in my mind that is enforcing this spirit into my life, in Jesus' name.

I renounce every evil covenant that I've come in contact with knowingly or unknowingly concerning witchcraft and rebellion, in Jesus' name.

I renounce every claim of the enemy over my life in the name of Jesus.

> By the blood of Jesus I wipe away every evil
> mark that has been placed upon me in the
> realm of the spirit, in Jesus' name.

Now as you begin to pray this prayer, this is how everything begins to unravel in the network that the enemy has placed around you and inside your soul. You will start having dreams, visions, and perceptions unlock in which God will begin to speak to you and show you things that need to be dealt with.

As I began to pray this prayer, God took me in the spirit one night and I stood before an army of my old action figures I had as a child. I looked down upon them on the floor and I just began to laugh, like, "What are you doing, an army formation?" The moment I laughed, the projection of witchcraft, heaviness, and attack that they carried was pushed against me so violently that I took it seriously as a formidable enemy. The moment I came back, I immediately went upstairs into the attic, got the box of toys, went outside, and burned them.

You might ask, "Why did you burn the toys?" When Paul was preaching in Acts 19:19, the demonstration of deliverance from demons was happening. The Bible says many of the people brought their witchcraft books together and burned them before all men. This is when I started understanding that certain items can resist you in your level of freedom, your level of prosperity, and your level of dominion. This is why it's so important not to open yourself up to items, clothing, movies, and music that are fueled by this spirit. It doesn't fly with God for you to say, "I'm just doing it for entertainment." You can't sit there and say, "I'm watching *Harry Potter* because it's entertainment." What you don't realize is that you have been initiated into witchcraft unknowingly. There are certain things that can never be sanctified. Even I have had to repent for movies, music, or certain things that I had no clue were opening me up to that spirit. Once you have the knowledge of good and evil, the knowledge of what you should be doing, God holds you accountable if you don't do it.

Breaking Demonic Assignments

The next level of witches are the witches who serve demons like we serve God. For example, these people openly practice magical arts and witchcraft for spiritual purposes. They are not your blind ones who just stumble unknowingly into witchcraft through entertainment like *Harry Potter* or other open doors. No, these witches actually practice sacrifices, séances, moon rituals—you name it. What I found extremely hilarious yet sad at same time is that those who practice Wicca don't even believe that they are serving the devil. Those who are the church of satan say they don't even believe in satan—they just believe in what he represents. I find that to be a blatant lie considering that these covens and true satanists perform rituals and blood sacrifices to invoke him. One of the things that satanists know is that if you want to get satan's attention, you have to get satan's attention. The top way of getting satan's attention is through child sacrifice—abortion. This is why anyone who works as an abortionist or has a job in the facility is 100 percent possessed.

No question about it. But this is also the place of high-level occult activity and satanism operating under the protection of the government. There have been many testimonies of satanic covens operating inside of the clinics because of what the sacrifice does in getting the devil's attention.

What I am about to share with you may shock some of you, but honestly, it's normal when you carry the anointing. This is one of hundreds of instances inside the church when I have confronted witches. We had a very powerful service in Orlando, Florida, and about 20 minutes into worship God began to speak to me about a particular lady who was in the crowd. Now, this happens all the time with words of knowledge, but I was contemplating saying to God, "We just started worship—I don't want to break the flow right now to speak to somebody." But no matter what, I could not shake the feeling that there was something not right. As I began to look at her, I saw in the spirit that this person was a practicing witch and had a man sitting beside her who was under a spell. He looked like a zombie. This was not some homeless couple coming in from the street—no, these were very nicely dressed Americans.

God has given me wisdom over the years. In my early days, I would have confronted them very sternly, looking for a battle. As I began to get closer to God, I started to realize that God loves them and wants to see them repent. There's a different way of approaching it from that standpoint. I began to walk toward her during the middle of worship. I bent over with the microphone behind my back, and I said, "Is it OK if I pray for you?"

She looked at me terrified and said, "Absolutely not. I only pray to my father."

That situation could have unfolded two different ways. If she would have humbled herself and repented, God would have delivered her and it would have been a powerful testimony. But because she chose to resist and literally fight the atmosphere, that turned on a different gear of warfare in me. I pointed at her and I said, "You came here with an assignment and you're exposed." I didn't throw her out like I once might have done, because her assignment was already exposed. In the environment and atmosphere of the power and the fire of God, God would be the one to turn up the temperature for her.

You see, God's power is fire. It is not a fantasy. It is a physical, tangible thing that can be felt in the natural. When it is needed just like with Elijah and the prophets of Baal, it is a very dangerous thing to deal with and try to come up against because it's up to God how high He turns the heat. I have seen people completely taken out because of resisting and fighting against the anointing on my life. In the Old Testament, God would use His prophets in very powerful demonstrations that would often result in people's deaths. Because we live under the new covenant of grace, many of those demonstrations ended through the blood of Jesus Christ, but this does not mean that God does not play. An example is in Acts with Ananias and Sapphira, who lied to Peter and to the Holy Spirit. As soon as they lied to him, they fell down dead before him. This is the New Testament. The same power exists today, but there are not many vessels who carry that level of authority.

This witch had been exposed, so I went back to worshiping but kept my eye on her. It didn't take 30 seconds before she began to shake, and she jumped up with the man beside her and they ran out the building. The moment that happened, my wife said on stage, "I don't know what just happened but I felt that a spirit of witchcraft just left this place." She did not know what had taken place, so it was a very powerful demonstration of what God can do when you walk in His wisdom and His power. The moment that witch ran out of the building, the atmosphere went to a new dimension and the power of God began to deliver people left and right.

It turned out that Charles Manson's grandson was in this service. He came up to me and I prayed with him and the power of God began to touch his life and deliver him. So there was a contention in the atmosphere for domination. Many dedicated witches and satanists will come and test you at your services if you carry the supernatural. Remember, they are drawn to the supernatural. They have to see that God's power is stronger than theirs. I have been in many situations when witches have repented and God has shown mercy. I have been in many other situations when they did not and their outcome was destruction.

CHAPTER 4

COVENANTS, CURSES, AND HOW TO OVERCOME

On our spiritual path with God, there must be congruency and there must be alignment with the Spirit. How can two walk together lest they agree? They cannot. We are going to discuss how to discern your circle and really destroy any assignment in the spirit realm that's coming against you. When God begins to unveil it or show you a dream or give you an impression or discernment, you still have to deal with this in the spirit. God will protect you. God will deliver you. God will prosper you and move you forward, but you still have to deal with what's happening and the junk that is going on behind the scenes.

The Enemy's Plans

We are going to first examine the topic—of the enemy's plans and schemes against the people of God. The Bible says that "*we are not ignorant of his devices*" (2 Corinthians 2:11 NKJV). God has a counterpoint of action for every attack of the enemy in order that satan might not outwit or outsmart us and take advantage of us, for we are not ignorant of his devices, his schemes, or his designs. God gives us the ability to identify and overcome the schemes of the enemy. The Word declares that we should not be outwitted by satan. There are many variables to how he attacks believers through schemes and through different designs. We must have the ability to discern these things.

We overcome the enemy's plots through prayer, fasting, and seeking God and His kingdom. We must make sure that we keep ourselves in an environment saturated in the presence of God, in the Word, and in His Spirit. When we live in that atmosphere, when these schemes or devices come against us, we know how to deal with them because God has revealed it.

God reveals the plot of the enemy in your circle and the people around you. Listen and pay attention to the words that are coming out of their mouths, because in time God will begin to reveal the motives of their heart. Out of the abundance of the heart, the mouth speaks. You may say, "Oh, you know, this person sounds fine," but if you step back and stay quiet for a little bit and listen to what they are really saying, the Lord can reveal their heart and motives to you. As you just listen, things will begin to be revealed because out of the belly flows the rivers of life. The Bible also says that out of the abundance of the heart, the mouth speaks.

Everything someone shares with you matters. Pay attention, especially when they say, "Oh, I'm just playing, I'm just joking around, I'm just messing with you." There is some truth to what they are saying to you. Deep down somewhere, they are speaking of out the wells of their heart. Oftentimes, they may not even recognize it themselves. But their words will always tell the truth. The way they think and feel is lying deep in their heart. You may call somebody a friend who is not really a friend. That's why I always ask God to remove every unfriendly friend of God around me. They can call themselves a friend, but God begins to reveal the true nature.

Sometimes the enemy will place someone along your path because blessings can come in a new season in the form of people. Curses can also come in a new season when someone can try to thwart the assignment of God on your life. They're actually a distraction to your life. When God blesses you, He often sends a person. When the enemy tries to trip you up and lay a trap for you, he often sends a person. So always look at the signs and ask God to truly reveal the motive of their hearts. That's one way to discern.

Let's pray over this topic of discernment and revealing the enemy's schemes:

> Father, I pray in the name of Jesus that You begin to move powerfully in Your people. I ask that You'll begin to speak to them about who is around them in their circle of friends and company. We ask You to reveal right now anyone who needs to be removed from our inner circle and from a place of influence. We thank You, God, that the blessing of the Lord comes to make us rich and You add no sorrow to it. I thank You right now for the gift of godly people who are in my corner. Thank You for the God-sent people who have pure hearts and are true friends. I bless them in the name of Jesus. I ask that You reveal any inner motives and hidden agendas that are in the hearts of the people in my circle. Show me the secret schemes of the enemy.

God can literally frustrate you to help lead you and reveal things to you. Let me explain the importance of your inner circle. Now, this is not addressing new believers who are coming out from a worldly lifestyle and groups of people who are still in the world and away from God. Absolutely there are people who cannot continue to be an integral part of your life if they are only serving themselves and running after the enemy. I'm talking about believers who have been in Christ for years, attending church, serving God, and still experiencing resistance in some areas of their life. There may be some people around you who are not for you. Let me tell you something—there are many witches in the church. Many warlocks are operating in a suit and tie every Sunday. They may love the Lord, but internally the systems of satan are functioning in their life. They have accepted Christ in their heart, but because they have refused to receive deliverance, the systems of rebellion and the engines of the enemy are flowing through them and so they are a defeated Christian.

The issue is that these mixed people are Christians, so when you look at them it's not necessarily the person who comes in with a black hood or any outward sign that they are operating in witchcraft. No, it can be very hidden and subtle. It's Brother A and Sister B sitting there clapping their hands, but because of the internal system of rebellion within them they're fighting against the vision of God in you. They are fighting against the purposes of God in you. I can put one foot inside of a church and that night the witch operating in that church will visit me and say, "What are you doing? I own this territory!" This happened in South Carolina. God showed me a person I didn't know—I met them once. Our second time at that church, this person said to me, "Oh, you're powerful," and we began to fight in the spirit. So I knew that this person was blocking the atmosphere in their church—yet they were on the church board. They were on the worship team. When you don't have discernment, you don't even know when people with internal systems of satan are fighting the atmosphere of freedom in your life. Motive is huge.

As mentioned earlier, out of the abundance of the heart the mouth speaks. So the overflow is what makes its way up to your mouth. The Bible says that you will be judged for every word you speak, every idle word, and every word that comes out of your mouth. God will look at and analyze and weigh it. So you hear people's hearts when they speak. When I hear people speak, I can tell motives. I can pick up the spirit behind it. God will always reveal people's intentions or motives when contrary to His purposes or plans. He will show the assignment against us or against the ministry by how people carry themselves in their words. You may be praying, "God, help me, deliver me," and God will reveal it through their own mouth. That why I said if you stay quiet for a little bit, seek God, and pray in the Spirit, the Lord will expose that thing.

When you ask God to expose every hidden agenda, He will even begin to expose the curses that people have released against you because sometimes you don't know what's spoken about in secret. They may be your friend when they are next to you, but in secret they're planning your downfall. They are setting a trap for you. They are digging a pit for you. In the name of Jesus, every pit that the enemy is digging for you—may they fall into their own pit (see Psalm 57:6). That pit of destruction is powerful. They are proud and they set a net for your feet, but may they be caught in it themselves, in the name of Jesus. Declare that you will fight back against every evil arrow, every curse and accusation of slander that was fired against you. All of this is to hinder your progress. All of it is a distraction to stop you from moving forward.

God will reveal what is spoken in secret to your ears. People don't really understand that when someone is a prophet or an apostle, they carry a powerful gift. I can be here in my office or in my car and I can hear your conversation at your dinner table. God can open my ears to hear actual conversations. God will open things up so you can see what's happening behind the scenes. It happens all the time with me. I'll hear conversations about what's going on or what people are thinking. In the natural, things look normal, but a few weeks later that situation will manifest. I have personally experienced this many times. God will warn you by His Spirit. Psalm 57:6 (NKJV) says, *"They have prepared a net for my steps; my soul is bowed down, they have dug a pit before me; into the midst of it they themselves have fallen."*

The very same trap the enemy is digging for you, God can cause him to fall into. Jealousy digs a pit. The spirit of jealousy comes against the work of God in your life when people begin to speak curses against you. Whenever anyone speaks, it is either a blessing or a curse. So when you see someone joking, begin to take that into consideration. If you're asking, "How do I separate myself from people who do that?" You just do it. You just separate yourself. You do not have time to be around a person who is sitting there speaking negatively, releasing curses on you. You are called to be blessed. You are called to set the captives free! You don't want to sit under a curse. You don't want to sit under oppression. God will begin to expose those things in Jesus' name.

Ecclesiastes 10:20 (NKJV) says, *"Do not curse the king."* Let's look at the King James Version: *"Curse not the king, no not in thy thought; and curse not the rich in thy bedchamber: for a bird of the air shall carry the voice, and that which hath wings shall tell the matter."* You have to be very careful. This could be for you if you need to understand how to be mature with your mouth. You don't want the enemy to use your words against you because you said something out of immaturity. We all grow. We all learn. We all have gossiped and we all have said negative things. As you mature, you will grow to a place where you will no longer do those things. You will be mindful of your words. Be careful, because when God reveals to you the plans of the enemy He'll begin to whisper what's going on so that you can deal with it. It takes maturity to know the plans of the enemy and deal with them in the proper way. A person may look normal, but in reality you cannot trust someone who has extreme jealousy or insecurity. That is a very dangerous place, but you can still love them.

Jealousy is serious and can cause people to do harmful things. You need to be careful how you navigate it, especially when people are not aligned with you—people who are not in right standing with God or are not living a righteous way. Jealousy can cause them to seek out other things and begin to make demonic covenants. They seek a different way to get rich or succeed over their peers, not in keeping with the ways of God, and so they make a demonic covenant. Serving demonic spirits goes hand in hand with jealousy, blinding a person and driving them to make ungodly decisions and agreements.

For example, my parents may have done something back in the day that made a demonic covenant because they wanted to succeed. My wife is also Haitian, so we have some firsthand experience with witchcraft. I've even heard of some Haitian churches that wanted their church to grow and actually made a pact with the enemy, saying that they did it in order for three to four generations of growth. The sin of that covenant needs to be broken. This is a real problem and has to be dealt with. Some of you may have given your life to Christ but wonder, *What is holding me down?* It is demonic, generational covenants that need to be broken.

GENERATIONAL CURSES

Generational curses and covenants carry power and have to be cut off or they will continue to impact your family. Exodus 20:5 (KJV) says, *"Thou shalt not bow down thyself to them, nor serve them: for I the Lord thy God am a jealous God, visiting the iniquity of the fathers upon the children unto the third and fourth generation of them that hate me."* What does it mean when it says "them that hate me"? Those are people who don't love God because they are not seeking God. They are living in wickedness. If you are living in wickedness, you cannot tell me you love God. If you love God, you will be all in for Him, and your will be toward Him and not worshiping your idol.

Some people think worshiping an idol means literally standing in front of a physical object and giving it glory. There is so much more to idol worship. Anything you and your family serve aside from God is an idol. Somewhere in your bloodline, your parents or your father or grandmother probably served something other than the true and living God. They made a pact in order to obtain something— wealth, success, health, whatever. They made a covenant with the enemy, exchanging something for something else, sacrificing something of value in exchange for power. It can be your hobby, your family, your spouse, your kids, your job, your appearance, or your image. This is a contract in the realm of the spirit. It can be a contract in the physical realm as well. Idolatry may not be just worshiping a statue. You may be watching Netflix eight hours a day. Your idol becomes Netflix. You've submitted your life to it. An idol is anything overtaking you.

We also need to analyze the high places mentioned in the Old Testament. A high place is any type of exalted place consecrated to God or an idol. God has really spoken to me a lot over this last year about high places in the spirit and how to deal with them. We have to deal with any high place in our lives that has resurrected itself. Even if you don't know what it is, the Holy Spirit will begin to remind you to adjust or balance that area. If it doesn't make sense, you can ask the Holy Spirit to help you identify any area that is under the influence of a high place. You can pray a simple prayer for that, something like this:

> Father, in the name of Jesus remove every high place in my mind and in my soul. Anything I've resurrected as a monument in rebellion against You, I reject it and I renounce it in the name of Jesus. I surrender myself

100 percent totally to Your Spirit and to Your kingdom in Jesus' name. Thank You, Lord.

If there are covenants that your parents made, they could be messing with you now, and you may be asking why this is happening. It's because the enemy has legal access and a legal right into your life. There's an open door. If you have not renounced this open door, it still has legal access. Sometimes this involves renouncing its claim on your life. Sometimes it takes some physical deliverance—someone needs to actually take you through the process of deliverance for you to become free of this high place. The thing is, God always brings these things to light if you have a willing and listening heart. If you're really intentional about being delivered, He will make you aware. He'll bring it to your memory.

My wife comes from a Haitian background. Her dad served heavily in voodoo and the occult. She remembers him saying that he built her childhood home, and in the house he made a covenant with these spirits that his children would serve him. Her sisters would get attacked heavily through demonic manifestations. Spirits held them down at night and during the day. At one point they were hospitalized because people thought they were crazy—because of this open door. One of her sisters thought that she had to serve this spirit to get relief from the torment, so she went back to Haiti to serve this spirit. She didn't get freedom—just more torment. When you try any way other than Jesus, demons can torment you because of demonic generational covenants in high places. The only deliverance is through

Jesus. The power in the blood of Jesus is the only way to be set free.

When people come under a generational covenant like that, it has to be broken. So when God set my wife free and delivered her, she began to renounce a lot of things. You need Jesus to give you freedom. When you get freedom from the enemy, he goes crazy. You may feel like "I just want to stop doing what I'm doing so that I'm not tormented anymore." But that's the lie of the enemy—you have to see it through. Once you start the process, you must see it through—there's no other option. Sometimes it takes a few months to get completely cleaned out and free.

With fasting and prayer and consistency, you can come to a place of total freedom, because God is molding you. When you start doing this over and over, you might start to associate your progress with the warfare. I did that when I went through 700-some days of encounters over two years—every single night, demonic encounters. I said, "This is not my life! I hate this! This is crazy!" And then one day it stopped and I said, "Oh my God, I'm not progressing," because I associated progress in the spirit with the warfare I was experiencing.

God spoke to me and said, "No, that season's over. You had to build a résumé in the spirit. Now you're recognized in the spirit." I had to build that résumé so that the enemy understood the dominion that I was carrying. So eventually the attacks will still happen, but it won't be every single night. You deal with it from that perspective.

DREAM COMMUNICATION

Let's discuss dreams for a moment. It's so important that you start looking at your dreams from a new perspective. There's a lot of teaching on dreams and the spirit world. Dreams are important to pay attention to, and God will reveal their meaning to you. Dreams mainly deliver what's happening. Often they are God teaching you as well as sometimes warning you. People get motivated when something starts to happen, and that's when they get up and pray and come against it. That's God revealing to you the assignment of the enemy. It is better to see it than not see it. When you begin to expel things, cleansing begins to happen. That's God delivering you from something; you may not know what that something was, but deliverance is taking place.

God begins to show you things and bring things to your remembrance. All of a sudden, you may hear your parents talking about something from your childhood. Sometimes you can ask your parents or relatives about your family history and why they moved to certain locations or did certain routines or celebrations. When I went back to Florida, I asked my mom about some things God was revealing to me. I was shocked by some of the things that she brought up. She said I would be shocked to see what God had protected me from in my life and that He led me to be a minister.

In conjunction with paying attention to your dreams, you should pray every single day. I would say 95 percent of my daily prayer time is praying in the spirit. You can only do so much in the natural, with your own understanding, but the spirit knows all things. You want to make sure that you're constantly praying because the Bible says that when you're praying in your most holy faith you're edifying yourself. When you pray in the spirit, in your heavenly language, the Bible says you are building up your most holy faith by praying in the spirit. So you're bringing edification to your spirit man. You need to make sure that your prayer life revolves around both praying in the spirit and with understanding. As you pray in the spirit, you will receive declarations for your life and words of knowledge and impressions of what to say in the natural. That's how you're going to really tap into the mysteries of God. The Bible says when you pray in the spirit, you are speaking mysteries. You are unveiling mysteries of the kingdom and mysteries of the spirit realm.

If you are experiencing dreams in your life, God could be showing you that you have got to learn how to fight. One of the things that I've been teaching for many years is how to really destroy the enemy in the spirit realm. In your dreams, you encounter the spirit realm and you have to engage and destroy. I want you to get those words in your system—*engage and destroy*. What does that mean? You need to train yourself in the natural so that whenever you go into a battle in the spirit, you are ready. You are going to be the aggressor in the spirit. You can never be the one who falls back. You can never be the one who takes a step back in fear. You lose instantly; all it takes is that first moment and you're done. You have to be the one who, when something is in front of you, goes on the offensive. You don't want to be on the defensive. You pursue.

The Bible says, "*The wicked flee when no one pursues, but the righteous are bold as a lion*" (Proverbs 28:1 NKJV). That internal stance is what we should hold to. God's going to test you in that. Some of you are still going around in circles, not fully operating in the dominion that God has given you because of fear. The enemy will keep testing you in these areas until you overcome. He has to recognize in you the spirit of someone who not only knows who they are in Christ but exercises the authority they have been granted through the revelation of identity.

As your pursuit of the Lord intensifies, boldness and authority is a byproduct of proximity to the Lord. It's not something that you have to wonder if it will be there or not. This is a direct correlation to your pursuit of Him. As you begin to do this when you experience an attack, the enemy will recognize that you're not one to mess with.

The enemy will keep at it. He will visit you and he'll know what you're afraid of. He will know when the door is open. He knows what time and what way to get to you. He knows that trigger and he looks for these little loopholes because he is a master of deception. He is a master illusionist. He wants to always make himself look bigger than God. So you have to train yourself from this moment that when you go into demonic encounters, you're just going to smile and attack like a madman. When you do that, witches in your region will fear you. Demons will look at you and say, "We can't mess with that one—they have an understanding."

Spiritual understanding is different from natural understanding. When you have a spiritual understanding of who you are, the position you walk in, the dominion that you're supposed to carry by the blood on the cross, you are viewed differently in the spirit. Once you see the victory happen, you build on that experience and grow in confidence in God. I taught our nine-year-old what to do when he is attacked. We talked about how to overcome these attacks. When a witch visited him, he said, "I rebuke you in the name of Jesus," and the witch shrank down to the size of a mouse and he started kicking it around. That's a little kid! That's victory!

VICTORY

Here's another testimony. I have a scar on my head—that scar is a victory. When I was 18 years old, I hit another car head-on going 80 miles per hour. My vehicle flipped into a tree and I was hanging out the window. It was a miracle I survived. When I walked away from the hospital that night, I barely had any marks on me. Many years later, as I started going through deliverance, I was renouncing things, and God took me in the realm of the spirit and dropped me in a house out in the middle of a winter wonderland. When you see snow, it can represent extreme warfare. That place was full of witches. They looked at me and began to battle and fight.

What I didn't mention is that God told me to remember a specific scripture: *"God is our refuge and strength, a very present help in trouble"* (Psalm 46:1 NKJV). The Holy Spirit said to me, "You must memorize this scripture by tonight," and I said, "Cool, all right." The level of depth in the realm of the spirit was not a dream. If I did not win in this encounter, I might not have woken up. That's the level of reality that I was in, and that's why God said, "You must remember this scripture."

When I went in the house in the winter wonderland, the witches pointed at me and at my scar. One of them said, "It's the one we tried to kill in the car wreck." As I began the battle, I began to feel choked and I was dying. I said, "God, I'm dying—what do I do?" Angels were looking down from heaven and they said, "What's the scripture?" I said, "Oh yes," and the moment I quoted that scripture, I was muscled like Samson. It was just crazy—my body just inflated and I defeated the witch and I got out of there. God showed me that assignment in the realm of the spirit. I had to overcome it. He didn't give me that ability on day one of my spiritual journey. This was after years of walking with God. He will put you in a battle where you have to be prepared or you will be destroyed.

Another scripture says, "*He will bring to light what is hidden in darkness and will expose the motives of the heart*" (1 Corinthians 4:5 NIV). When you pray and when you have the right motives, God will protect you. God will speak to you. The Bible says in Job 5:12 (NKJV), "*He frustrates the devices of the crafty, So that their hands cannot carry out their plans.*" He frustrates the plans of the crafty, the shrewd, and the schemers. Is anyone scheming against your life? God is going to frustrate their hands, in the name of Jesus.

> I declare right now that every scheme against your life is exposed from behind the scenes. May God begin to judge their hands right

now, in the name of Jesus. May God begin to expose their hands right now, in the name of Jesus. They shall not succeed against your life, in Jesus' name. They shall not succeed against your ministry and your household, in the name of Jesus. They shall not succeed. He frustrates the plans of the crafty, so their hands shall not succeed. They will not be able to carry out those demonic agendas or plans against you because God is exposing it, in the name of Jesus. Expose every plan. Expose every unfriendly friend. Expose every agent, in the name of Jesus. Let everything that's been crafted against you be destroyed by fire, in the name of Jesus.

REMAINING PURE IN HEART

Some people experience a sensation that someone is trying to call your soul out of your body. That is a summoning of your spirit. If it feels demonic, it may be a witch trying to summon your spirit. We cancel that assignment.

Every summoning of our spirit through our dreams, we command it to be destroyed right now in the mighty name of Jesus. There will be no summoning of spirit or heart on any altar, in Jesus' mighty name. We take back any of our belongings that are on any witchcraft altar, in the name of Jesus. May any witch or

> wizard who is trying to touch us catch fire, in Jesus' mighty name. May every plan of the enemy, every scheme, be destroyed. The works of their hands shall not prosper against us, in Jesus' name. The works of their hands shall not prosper against your life. They shall not prosper against your ministry. They shall not prosper against your children, in the name of Jesus. They shall not prosper against your finances, in the name of Jesus. They shall not prosper. God thwarts the plans of the crafty.

The Bible says the Lord searches the heart: *"For the righteous God tests the hearts and minds"* (Psalm 7:9 NKJV). He examines every secret motive. God will reward each person according to their conduct—according to what their deeds deserve. This is a spiritual principle. God is a God of love but also a God of righteous judgment. He weighs out the motives of the heart. It doesn't matter even if fellow believers are coming against you. God looks at them and says, "I will weigh out your motive, and if it's not right, you will get what you deserve."

That's why it's so important to keep a pure heart, even when people may be afflicting you or against you. You may be saying, "How can this happen? How can the people in the body of Christ do these things?" Maintain proper alignment. When you do that, God is watching. It doesn't matter what's going on in the natural—He's weighing hearts. That is what He does.

When Samuel was picking the king of Israel, God declared that He looks at the heart (see 1 Samuel 16:7). If you can keep your heart right before the Lord, He will always fight on your behalf. That's the secret. I've learned that the Lord of my life will fight my battles for me. He is watching over me. He will fight my battles and elevate me to new dimensions as long as I keep my heart right with Him. Even when I make mistakes, even when I do stupid things, as long as I maintain that humility He will fight for me.

David was the greatest king in the Bible because he knew how to repent. David made crazy mistakes in his life, really terrible mistakes, but because of his ability to humble himself, he was a great king in the Bible. It is so important to constantly lay your heart before the Lord. Constantly surrender and say, "Lord, deliver me from false and secret motives that the enemy may be driving within me. Deliver me from the motives of the flesh." This is how you live a life of victory.

CHAPTER 5

WHAT IS A FAMILIAR SPIRIT?

In layman's terms, a familiar spirit is a demon. First Samuel 28:7 says that Saul, the king of Israel, sought out a medium at Endor, who was said to have a familiar spirit. He went to her to perform a séance to call forth the prophet Samuel from the dead. A familiar spirit accompanies anyone *"who conjures spells, or a medium, or a spiritist, or one who calls up the dead"* (Deuteronomy 18:11 NKJV). Someone operating with a familiar spirit will practice magic spells and witchcraft. They also claim to contact the dead and have supernatural wisdom from supernatural sources.

A familiar spirit can have an assignment to survey and study people, territories, and bloodlines of families. Their assignment is to gather spiritual intelligence that will open doors to instigate destruction. They enter and gain power in people's lives by disguising themselves as something common (familiar) while operating through unaware people, places, and things. God has clearly warned His people about consulting with mediums or those with a familiar spirit:

> *When you come into the land which the Lord your God is giving you, you shall not learn to follow the abominations of those nations. There shall not be found among you anyone who makes his son or his daughter pass through the fire, or one who practices witchcraft, or a soothsayer, or one who interprets omens, or a sorcerer, or one who conjures spells, or a medium, or a spiritist, or one who calls up the dead. For all who do these things are an abomination to the Lord* (Deuteronomy 18:9-12 NKJV).

He instructed the children of Israel, "*Give no regard to mediums and familiar spirits; do not seek after them, to be defiled by them: I am the Lord your God*" (Leviticus 19:31 NKJV). By consulting the spirits of devils, men would become deceived by their lies. When King Saul cut himself off from God by his disobedience, he turned to demons for guidance. Saul resisted God, the source of life, and sought after the devil, which was absolute foolishness and led to his ultimate downfall.

The Bible tells us clearly that the living should not consult with the dead, for *"the dead know nothing"* (Ecclesiastes 9:5 NKJV). It also goes on to say that *"their love, and their hatred, and their envy, is now perished; neither have they any more a portion for ever in any thing that is done under the sun"* (Ecclesiastes 9:6 KJV). Satan will appear as an angel of light, and demons can appear as the dead. Furthermore, and even more shocking, the enemy will attempt to appear as Christ Himself: *"For false christs and false prophets will rise and show great signs and wonders to deceive, if possible, even the elect"* (Matthew 24:24 NKJV).

Any spirit claiming to be a deceased loved one is really a devil impersonating them. For this reason, God's people should reject any miracle worker who claims to receive special insight, revelation, or knowledge through contacting the spirits of the dead. The Lord instructed His children in Isaiah 8:19-20 (NKJV) regarding these types of spirits, saying:

> *And when they say to you, "Seek those who are mediums and wizards, who whisper and mutter," should not a people seek their God? Should they seek the dead on behalf of the living? To the law and to the testimony! If they do not speak according to this word, it is because there is no light in them.*

Isaiah directly addressed this issue and declared that mankind should steer away from the words of devils and turn back to God's words and His prophets, who bear His testimony. Believers should seek out the Scriptures as a guide to the truth and adhere to it as the standard for righteous living.

God has revealed Himself in His Word, and only through Him can there be peace and knowledge of the things to come or the future. If anyone claims to carry a supernatural power from spirits or claims they have knowledge of the future outside of the Holy Spirit, they have no light within them. Nobody who claims that they speak to the dead is speaking to the dead. These are demons masquerading as relatives or people who have passed on. They gain entrance because of an emotional connection or relationship.

Another type of familiar spirit operates by searching your family history, just like someone performing a Google search of your name. Familiar spirits have access to what has transpired in the natural. They have information and history from your family genealogy. When the enemy begins to search your family history, he is looking for any type of iniquity in your bloodline. If you had ancestors who had a proclivity toward alcoholism or any type of addiction, the enemy will grab hold of that area as an entry point of attack. The enemy searches the bloodline for the easiest and quickest link in order to infiltrate your life. This concept is recognized in the medical field as well—physicians want to know your family medical history because diseases and health issues are hereditary. Likewise, certain iniquities are passed down in the bloodline through the "family tree."

When we consistently renounce iniquity in our deliverance process, we remove all legal right of the enemy to access us through those easy entry points. These entry points are not due to an individual's own actions or invitations to the spirit world, but are simply part of their makeup as a person. Whenever I am teaching on deliverance, I always begin with this foundational standpoint. This prayer is crucial and one of the first steps to being set free from the influence of the enemy.

PRAYER OF ACTIVATION

I RENOUNCE ALL INIQUITY IN MY BLOODLINE, IN THE NAME OF JESUS.

I RENOUNCE EVERY CLAIM OF THE ENEMY OVER MY LIFE, IN JESUS' NAME.

I RENOUNCE EVERY SPIRIT THAT IS CALLING MY NAME THROUGH MY BLOODLINE, IN THE NAME OF JESUS.

I RENOUNCE ANY EVIL COVENANT I HAVE MADE KNOWINGLY OR UNKNOWINGLY, IN THE NAME OF JESUS.

As you pray this prayer, you are literally breaking up fallow ground in the spirit. As this begins to happen, do not be surprised by manifestations in your body or your mind. This is a great step because you are removing the legal access satan has to your life. As you follow this process, God will begin to show you prophetic visions and dreams. He will show you how to deal with more in-depth places of bondage in your life specifically.

For example, if you begin to pray these prayers and God continues to shows you visions of being underwater, alligators, water serpents, or anything of that nature, this is an indication that the marine kingdom is fighting your life very strongly. This is the most stubborn resistance in the kingdom of satan. This is where perversion, seduction, pride, fame, financial attack, or financial gain through making a deal with the devil all take place. The marine kingdom is a place where specific perfumes, colognes, cosmetics, styles of dress, and dances have come from. We'll dive deeper into the marine kingdom a little later in this book.

Am I saying we should not have any of these things? Absolutely not, you just have to be discerning. If God is showing you these specific dreams or visions, then this is an area that needs to be addressed in prayer and fasting in your personal life.

As you renounce iniquity, God shows you strike areas of the enemy's attack against your life. What you have to do is specifically go into prayer warfare against what God has shown you until you see victory. What does victory look like? God will show you in a dream and a vision; He will give you confirmation. He will confirm it through other men and women of God. These attacks will decrease until they no longer occur. As you begin to deal with the foundational issues of iniquity and covenants, make sure you are very aware of what you see in the spirit and what God shows you in dreams and visions. Take action in prayer and fasting so you can overcome and walk in total freedom.

CHAPTER 6

DIVINATION: THE PYTHON SPIRIT

Acts 16:16 (NKJV) says, *"Now it happened, as we went to prayer, that a certain slave girl possessed with a spirit of divination met us, who brought her masters much profit by fortune-telling."* The original Greek word *pythonos* translated is a spirit of divination. Literally, the Greek word in this text means "a spirit of Python." In historical paganism, Python was said to be a serpent in southern Greece that had the power of divination. To understand the depth of this, we have to recognize that there are two sources of spiritual power. One source is the living God, who is omnipresent, omniscient, all powerful, ruler of heaven and earth. The other source is satan—a fallen angel and a creature whose spiritual power pales in comparison to the Creator. Satan can only mimic or counterfeit what has already been created by God Himself.

The demon in the slave girl drew power from satan and said things about the future that came to pass so frequently that it brought her masters much profit by fortune-telling. If we were to break down this one sentence alone, hopefully this will open the eyes of many of you. Forth-telling and prophetic accuracy are not the be-all end-all. As a matter of fact, many of you could be in situations where you need deliverance because you received a word that was accurate but did not originate from God. There are many prophetic people in the church who are full of mixture. There are many prophetic voices who are defiled. Knowing whom to glean from should be a number-one focus as a believer.

My wife and I have always been very cautious about who we glean from and who we will receive from in the spirit. Over the years, we have allowed only a handful of these people in our lives. Sadly, the prophetic movement that is happening in the church now is full of devils. I hate to say it, but some of your favorite preachers are among them. They have giftings, but because they have not followed the course of holiness, mixture has set in. You have so many prophetic voices running around doing more damage than good. The Bible says in Acts 16:17-18 (NKJV):

> *This girl followed Paul and us, and cried out, saying, "These men are the servants of the Most High God, who proclaim to us the way of salvation." And this she did for many days. But Paul, greatly annoyed, turned and said to the spirit, "I command you in the name of Jesus Christ to come out of her." And he came out that very hour.*

What did the slave girl who was possessed by divination call out? *"These men are the servants of the Most High God, who proclaim to us the way of salvation."* Was she correct? Absolutely. In Acts 16:18, it says Paul was greatly annoyed for at least three reasons. First, she followed them around and kept repeating this for many days. Second, crying this out during prayer was probably a great disturbance. Third, when people confirmed that these men indeed were the servants of the Most High God who proclaimed the way of salvation, I guarantee that many of them were at risk because they trusted the words of this girl and the demon working through her.

Today, psychics, witches, and fortune tellers are also empowered by this same spirit that says things that come to pass. What is sad and crazy is that many ministers today lack the discernment of spirits and would probably have made this girl an evangelist on their staff because she kept crying out and declaring something that sounded correct, like an evangelist does! This is why discerning of spirits is so vital in the church today. I believe it took many days for Paul to really unravel the revelation of what was going on and to discern and recognize this was not a spirit of God. You see, when your discernment is active, you may feel, recognize, or even get a specific word for a situation, but you may not have the full understanding. Sometimes it takes time for your discernment to completely unveil a situation with an answer. By grace, Paul continued ministering as she followed them. I imagine in his mind he was thinking, "Well, this is exactly true, but there's something off." The Bible says that Paul was irked in his spirit. Factual information does not mean the original source is the correct spirit.

The Bible says there is the spirit of truth and the spirit of error. You can have factual information and still be in a spirit of error. God says seeking advice from psychics, witches, and fortune tellers—he calls them abominations— is strictly forbidden.

> *When you come into the land which the Lord your God is giving you, you shall not learn to follow the abominations of those nations. There shall not be found among you anyone who makes his son or his daughter pass through the fire, or one who practices witchcraft, or a soothsayer, or one who interprets omens, or a sorcerer, or one who conjures spells, or a medium, or a spiritist, or one who calls up the dead. For all who do these things are an abomination to the Lord, and because of these abominations the Lord your God drives them out from before you. You shall be blameless before the Lord your God.*

For these nations which you will dispossess listened to soothsayers and diviners; but as for you, the Lord your God has not appointed such for you (Deuteronomy 18:9-14 NKJV).

Give no regard to mediums and familiar spirits; do not seek after them, to be defiled by them: I am the Lord your God (Leviticus 19:31 NKJV).

And the person who turns to mediums and familiar spirits, to prostitute himself with them, I will set My face against that person and cut him off from his people (Leviticus 20:6 NKJV).

Seeking guidance from any spiritual source other than God and the Holy Spirit whom Jesus has sent is an abomination and idolatry before God.

GUARDING YOUR DREAMS

Now let's talk about a very powerful subject—interpreting witchcraft attacks in your dreams. Unfortunately, most do not understand how to deal with this, yet it is one of the most important aspects of your Christian walk. Everyone has dreams. You will live a defeated life if you do not take into account the significance of the dream world. God clearly speaks to us in dreams and visions. It is often easiest to communicate with mankind in dreams because the person is asleep. Let's really take a deep dive into this area to give you an understanding of why this happens.

Because of the hectic day-to-day schedule and the busyness of life, many different variables weigh people down spiritually while they are awake. It is easier to reach an individual who is at complete rest and begin to speak to them or reveal danger signs to them. It is also a time when the enemy works as well. While we sleep, the enemy comes in and begins to plant thoughts, seeds, and demonic systems to try and come against your life in the natural. These things are created in the spirit realm, and you see the manifestation happen in the natural. This is why it's extremely important never to just bypass or shrug off what you see in your dreams. God is constantly speaking to you. He is constantly warning you through them.

One of the secrets to a powerful, victorious life in the spirit is to continually die to our flesh. The more crucified the flesh, the easier it is to see in the spirit and to have encounters, visitations, and supernatural experiences. Let's take it a step further and see what crucifying the flesh means. When you begin to crucify the flesh, you are literally increasing your spirit man's ability to interpret and encounter the spirit world.

Here are two examples of the power of crucifying the flesh. The first example is a familiar picture of what it means to be consecrated—a Buddhist monk. Buddhist monks will stay in deep meditation, focusing in order to access the spirit realm. These people are extremely deep and carry a demonic force behind them. They have entered the spirit realm illegally. Because of the principles of crucifying the flesh by fasting and meditation, they open a door of access. The reason the Western church is dead in spirit is because they gratify the flesh more than they crucify it. They do not do anything that allows their spirit man to be built up and become perceptive. You will never demonstrate God's power and anointing or have spiritual authority and influence by being a glutton. You will never carry true revival within your heart by fasting once every few months. Every believer has been granted the ability to walk in an extreme dimension of authority in the spirit, but that doesn't happen just because you accept Christ.

The second example of dying to self is Jesus. Even Jesus knew that the spiritual laws that God placed here on earth were required of Him. The Bible says Jesus fasted for 40 days before He walked in extreme dominion. The first thing Jesus did before any single act of power was to be led by the Spirit of God into the wilderness to be tempted by the devil. Jesus made a choice to obey, go into the wilderness, and fast and pray. This is the pivotal moment that allowed Jesus to come out in the power of the Spirit.

The Buddhist monk accessed the spirit realm illegally, but because he crucified the flesh by fasting and meditation, he still entered in. On the flip side, we see that Jesus was led by the Spirit into the wilderness to fast for 40 days in order to come out in the power of the Spirit. True power is demonstrated by vessels who have placed themselves in a position of crucifying the flesh in many ways. For example, reading your Bible, praying, and worshiping—all of these are examples of crucifying the flesh and edifying your spirit man. Each one of them carries a different level of impact.

Fasting carries a higher level of impact because you are literally denying your body what it needs to physically survive. When you fast and deny yourself, you are opening yourself up to the spirit realm. Now with this revelation, your motive must be correct. There must be holiness in applying these principles. Power is not demonstrated by people who have not crucified their flesh—whether good or bad. As you can see with the Buddhist monk, he is applying principles that are correct, but because they are infiltrated by demons, he is operating in error. But this does not take away from the fact that he does indeed facilitate demonic power and forces. This is why so many people are led astray by the occult or satanism, because they truly demonstrate power. They truly demonstrate a measure of authority given to them by the devil.

I want to lay out the five pillars that will help you win every battle in the realm of the spirit. A pillar is something that holds up a building—it is part of the foundation. In the New Testament, Jesus gave us a very powerful statement about overcoming the storms and the wind. The storms and the wind represent our battles and the trying situations that we face in life. Jesus said, "*Therefore whosoever heareth these sayings of mine, and doeth them, I will liken him unto a wise man, which built his house upon a rock*" (Matthew 7:24 KJV). Jesus is referring to the house as a representation of someone's spiritual life and wellbeing. This is why it's very important that when you have dreams of a home, you take note of the structure of the home. If it is well-built, is it big or is it small? The Lord is giving prophetic insight into your spiritual atmosphere. If you have a dream of a rundown home, you have some work to do. If you have a dream of a mansion, this doesn't necessarily mean that God is going to give you a mansion in the natural, but it does show that you are doing very well in the spirit. These five pillars are crucial for every believer to adhere to if they want to see victory in their life.

PILLAR NUMBER ONE: THE WORD OF GOD

Let's begin with the foundation, which is the Word of God. These pillars are not necessarily in order of importance, but all the other pillars hinge on this—the Word. Romans 10:17 (NKJV) says, "*So then faith comes by hearing, and hearing by the word of God.*" You need to understand that in order to function in the faith arena, the Word must be in your heart. It is impossible to live in faith if the Word of God is not in your system. You must live and breathe the Word of God. It is the foundation upon which everything is established. Without the foundation of the word, nothing else we talk about matters. God's Word is a living, breathing organism. It is His breath in written form. The Bible says that the sword of the spirit is the Word of God. Can you imagine going into battle with no sword? Can you imagine enrolling into the military and your instructor sending you to battle without even showing you how to use your weapon?

Unfortunately, many Christians have become casualties of spiritual war. There can be so much emphasis on spiritual gifting that believers get taken out by the enemy fairly quickly. They think the gifting trumps the need for the Word of God, and that is so far from the truth. The Word is the foundation and the amplifier of everything that will come forth from your life. It will sharpen you in ways unimaginable and open you up to the things of the spirit and the instruction of the Lord.

One of the very first times I was ever taken into the realm of the spirit was over 15 years ago. As I began to be taken into this encounter, I was holding a Bible. As I was looking at that Bible, electricity was sparking all around it. It sounded like static and looked like blue lightning. I lifted my head and in the distance and I saw many mountains in front of me. I took the Bible and swung it like a sword and leveled those mountains. During this time, I was a newbie in the things of the supernatural, so I didn't even understand that mountains could represent resistance and strongholds. God was giving me insight into how powerful His Word is as a weapon.

Immediately after those mountains had been leveled, I looked down at the Bible and it began to glow with a brilliant, piercing white light that would have blinded anyone in the natural. I immediately knew this was what Paul experienced on his way to Damascus. But since I was in the spirit, the light was not blinding me. I begin to hear all around me this massive drum-like sound, "Thump, thump, thump." I knew that this sound was coming from within the Bible. I was able to pierce through the light and see a physical heart that was beating within the Word. Immediately after seeing this, I heard an angel scream at the top of his voice, "It's alive!" The power of his voice shook me and catapulted me back to my body.

I woke up from this experience with a newfound revelation that I have carried my whole life—that the very heart of God is in the Word. The revelation that the Word is a living, breathing organism. This is found written in the Word in Hebrews 4:12 (ESV). It says, *"For the word of God is living and active, sharper than any two-edged sword."* Psalm 1:1-3 (ESV) says:

> *Blessed is the man who walks not in the counsel of the wicked, nor stands in the way of sinners, nor sits in the seat of scoffers; but his delight is in the law of the Lord, and on his law he meditates day and night. He is like a tree planted by streams of water that yields its fruit in its season, and its leaf does not wither.*

We must understand that this scripture shows that when we have the Word of God in us, we are planted by a river. Streams of water, which is the Spirit, will continually flow through us, making sure that we are bearing fruit. Nobody can bear fruit outside of Christ or His Spirit.

PILLAR NUMBER TWO: PRAYER

First John 5:14-15 (NKJV) says, *"Now this is the confidence that we have in Him, that if we ask anything according to His will, He hears us. And if we know that He hears us, whatever we ask, we know that we have the petitions that we have asked of Him."* Prayer is a vital weapon when it comes to spiritual warfare. Let's break down prayer in a very simplistic way. Prayer is the communication path between you and God.

It is what relationship is built upon. Just like the human language is used to build relationships between humans, and time is involved in communication in order to build that relationship, God speaks to us believers through prayer. We must understand it is not just about petitions or a wish list, which is sadly what most Christians have made prayer to be. Prayer is the communication pathway by which relationship is developed. Many believers have traded the personal intimacy of private prayer, which God wants, with the corporate setting as the main supplier of prayer. What does this mean? Prayer was meant to be in fellowship one on one. There are benefits to corporate prayer and coming into an agreement with a fellow believer, but prayer was intended to be the intimacy platform by which humans and God communicate. Many believers have given up personal prayer time because of laziness or ignorance.

We must make sure that we don't lose the emphasis upon prayer—communication between God and mankind—as a personal connection. How does this affect you in spiritual warfare? The closer you are to the Lord, the more His Spirit begins to lead and guide you into battle. Many Christians have become casualties of war because they simply do not understand how to engage the enemy in prayer. When we are facing a demonic assignment or an attack, we are to go into battle to deal with it. God is constantly speaking to us through dreams, visions, other people, and confirmations through signs and wonders around us to get His voice to us.

Dreams and visions are the most prominent place that you can recognize demonic assignments against you in the realm of the spirit. Once you have established that something has been released against you, you need to go into prayer. One of the things the Lord taught me many years ago was how to be victorious every single time I wage war. First, you take time repenting of all sin, declaring the blood of Jesus over yourself, and understanding that you are washed in His blood. I always start with repentance. I begin to repent for the lusts of the flesh, the lust of the eyes, and the pride of this life as declared in the Word. I begin to renounce these things. I begin to renounce ungodliness and worldly desire, which is also described in the Scriptures. I begin to renounce all iniquity. During this process, if there is something specific that the Lord brings to my attention, I deal with it immediately. I sense the release, and then it is time to press into warfare tongues.

As you begin to press into prayer, you are now no longer limited by any spot or wrinkle or heaviness of sin that can prevent impact and depth in the spirit. I begin to pray in tongues until God deposits a prayer point within my spirit. The Bible says that as I pray in an unknown tongue, my understanding is unfruitful yet I am speaking mysteries. The Bible also says that when I pray in an unknown tongue, I can also pray with my understanding. For example, as I begin to pray in the spirit, I will feel an emphasis, a vision, or a direction on what to pray. I will then declare that prayer point in my natural language and go right back into praying in tongues. I do this until I feel a release of peace or my next prayer point dropping into my spirit. Do not be alarmed if you go 15 or 20 minutes on one prayer point. You are making serious headway and going deep. Sometimes when I go into prayer, these prayer points begin to flow like water and I'm rapidly declaring different points throughout my prayer time.

Each prayer session is dictated by the flow of the Spirit. This is what you need to understand when it comes to dealing with demonic assignments and waging war against the plans of the enemy. Prayer warfare is essential.

PILLAR NUMBER THREE: FASTING

Now let's go into the gasoline that gets poured on the fire that's burning within you—fasting. Matthew 6:16-18 (NIV) says:

> *When you fast, do not look somber as the hypocrites do, for they disfigure their faces to show others they are fasting. Truly I tell you, they have received their reward in full. But when you fast, put oil on your head and wash your face, so that it will not be obvious to others that you are fasting, but only to your Father, who is unseen; and your Father, who sees what is done in secret, will reward you.*

Once you start understanding the biblical applications of fasting, satan will always try to hinder the depth and the power that is released upon you through this spiritual principle. This Scripture says not to be like the hypocrites, for they disfigure their faces to show men that they are spiritual. They want people to recognize them; they want people to look at them and say, "Whoa, those must be some serious holy men." They look for the praise of men. That is the essence of pride and is disgusting before God. *"Pride goes before destruction, a haughty spirit before a fall"* (Proverbs 16:18 NIV). The Bible says that this type of fasting that is done with pride receives its full reward by the applause of people, which gets you nothing in life! But when you fast the correct way, don't make your fasting obvious to people but only to your Father who is unseen. Your Father, who sees what is done in secret, will reward you openly.

Fasting is a spiritual principle that opens the door to the supernatural and flow of God's power. In Mark 2:18-20 (NKJV), Mark writes:

> *The disciples of John and of the Pharisees were fasting. Then they came and said to Him, "Why do the disciples of John and of the Pharisees fast, but Your disciples do not fast?" And Jesus said to them, "Can the friends of the bridegroom fast while the bridegroom is with them? As long as they have the bridegroom with them they cannot fast. But the days will come when the bridegroom will be taken away from them, and then they will fast in those days."*

We can get some really awesome revelation about fasting from this scripture. You can see how the question arose about the disciples of John the Baptist and the disciples of the Pharisees. Why is it that they were constantly fasting but the disciples of Jesus were not? We find the answer here: *"But the days will come when the bridegroom will be taken away from them, and then they will fast in those days."* There was no need for the disciples to fast because they were literally in the presence of Jesus. But we can see that after Jesus ascended on high, in order for the disciples to be in His presence, fasting must take place. The disciples were in close proximity and the Lord was constantly radiating around them as He was teaching them and pouring into them. Once He was taken away into glory, in order to have that type of fellowship, that intimacy, that type of connection, fasting is required.

The discipline of fasting crucifies the flesh so that the spirit man starts to arise. Whenever the flesh is crucified by abstaining from food or water, physical weakness starts to take place. This is the natural reaction of the body when fasting. When the physical body enters a weakened state, the spirit man is actually strengthened. Your ability to perceive and tap into the things of the spirit are extremely heightened. Fasting is a key that opens the door to the supernatural. Fasting is a key that accesses power.

Now there's a flip side to this as well. Fasting is a spiritual principle, so that means that anyone can open the door to the spirit realm and access power, even if the motives are wrong or if Christ is not the central focus. We see this with other religions like Buddhism and eastern mysticism. These people understand that they can access the spirit realm through fasting and meditation, although they are being driven by a demonic spirit. They have the ability to obtain substance. This substance is demonic in nature, but because the principle of fasting is true and it opens the door to the spirit realm, it doesn't matter if the individual is a believer or not.

It has always blown my mind to see the unbeliever have more spiritual discipline in fasting than believers in the Western church. This is why you see people in other places, such as Africa, who are extremely powerful in the spirit because they understand the principle of fasting. As with anything, mixture can set in if the motives are not correct. The law of fasting that God set here on earth is truly a key that anyone can access.

When I began my journey of fasting, I remember I couldn't go more than a few hours on a fast because I was an athlete. I was used to constantly eating throughout the day. But I knew as I read the Scriptures that God was leading me deeper into His presence. I knew that in order for me to carry true power, I would have to live a lifestyle of fasting. I'll never forget the first time I did a 24-hour fast—I felt the best I've ever felt in my life!

A short time after that, the Lord led me into a three-day fast, a seven-day fast, and then a few years later He led me to do a 40-day fast. When I did a 40-day fast is when I truly started operating in dominion. A 40-day fast is known as a dominion fast. I had crucified my flesh so much that the spirit realm became more real than the natural to me. I had to learn to balance what I was seeing, hearing, and operating in. As the Holy Spirit began to teach me how to function, I began to see explosive moves of God and signs and wonders break forth everywhere I went.

PILLAR NUMBER FOUR: WORSHIP

For the weapons of our warfare are not carnal but mighty in God for pulling down strongholds (2 Corinthians 10:4 NKJV).

Worshiping is one of the most powerful weapons we have as a believer, because as we worship, it is a sweet-smelling incense unto the Lord. Many people truly do not tap into the atmosphere of worship properly, because they have not crucified the flesh enough to focus on the Lord. This is a process of learning to surrender that will place you in such a deep dimension of His presence, nothing can compare to it. I remember many times in my life going so deep in worship that supernatural encounters would happen in the natural instantly. I had so many more visitations because of the atmosphere of worship that was being facilitated as a lifestyle in my life.

PILLAR NUMBER FIVE: PRAISE

In the story of Jehoshaphat in 2 Chronicles 20, the people began to sing and praise and the enemy was defeated.

Sometimes your key to breakthrough lies in your praise. The Bible says to put on *"the garment of praise for the spirit of heaviness"* (Isaiah 61:3 NKJV). We understand that not every key on our key chain opens every lock. My key for the car will not open up my house. It is the same with these pillars. Some pillars will open up a dimension of deliverance, freedom, or revelation that others may not. Praise is a weapon. It also positions us in the joy of the Lord. The Bible says that the kingdom of God is not meat and drink but righteousness, peace, and joy in the Holy Spirit. Many believers lack joy. They simply do not enjoy life, nor do they have the supernatural joy that comes through Christ. I guarantee if you would take a moment and dance your heart out, jump, shout, and praise—not for 30 seconds but for 30 minutes—your life will change this very moment. You're using a different key to unlock something in your life.

I gave this same prescription to a person in a very bad situation and within 30 minutes their whole life was delivered. They've taken what I shared with them and used it consistently from that moment forward. Sometimes we forget the Bible says the joy of the Lord is our strength. Do you need strength in your life? Start to praise Him; start to dance around with your heart completely focused on Him, and strength will enter your life. Look at David—he danced until his clothes fell off. He carried a lifestyle of praise, yet he was the greatest warrior in the Bible. You see that these two go hand in hand.

CHAPTER 7

PRAYERS OF THE FLESH

One of the things we have to be very conscious of is making sure that our prayers have not turned fleshly. James 4:1-6 (NIV) says:

> *What causes fights and quarrels among you? Don't they come from your desires that battle within you? You desire but do not have, so you kill. You covet but you cannot get what you want, so you quarrel and fight. You do not have because you do not ask God. When you ask, you do not receive, because you ask with*

wrong motives, that you may spend what you get on your pleasures. You adulterous people, don't you know that friendship with the world means enmity against God? Therefore, anyone who chooses to be a friend of the world becomes an enemy of God. Or do you think Scripture says without reason that he jealously longs for the spirit he has caused to dwell in us? But he gives us more grace. That is why Scripture says: "God opposes the proud but shows favor to the humble."

The Bible is clearly saying that we have not because we ask not. However, when we have learned to ask in prayer, we can end up asking incorrectly based on our own worldly desires and our own lusts. The Bible says that when we ask, we should be aware of our heart's motives. "*God opposes the proud but shows favor to the humble.*" This scripture is emphasizing prideful prayers, prayers of the flesh, and not prayers of humility of spirit. Wrong motives are the driving force of Christians who have mixture in their lives. Because the flesh is so alive in them and they have not crucified it through applying the pillars of spiritual discipline, they cannot rationally speak and pray things of the spirit because the flesh is ruling them. This is the type of broken Christian who is constantly complaining and murmuring, yet they believe that what they are saying or doing is right.

If we pray anything according to His will, He hears us, and if He hears us, we know we have what we ask (see 1 John 5:14). So we need to understand that prayer is just not about throwing up a wish list or desires but understanding the actual will of God. Until you can perceive God's will, you can never put that into prayer and see manifestations take place. When I learned this secret, I was in the professional sports industry, training celebrities and top-level athletes. Even in my gifting, which God had used to open doors to minister to influential people, I started to feel a frustration in the realm of the spirit that I was not fulfilling my assignment. I didn't recognize why I felt like I was dying on the inside when I was actually functioning in the gift that God had given me. As I began to pray and I found 1 John 5:14, I recognized that I must spend time in prayer to discover the will of God. I actually spent long hours in prayer, literally just pursuing His will.

Many believers have never even heard of this notion. Most Christians know and learn the Lord's Prayer and that's it! By spending time pursuing His will, you are then able to regurgitate that back into your personal prayer points for your life. This is one of the mysteries of seeing God move all the time in your life. We have to understand that it's about His will. As I began to pray in the early morning hours at the gym before clients came in, I pursued His will and His will only. In those moments, He began to reveal to me His plans for my life. He revealed to me that my assignment had to shift from what I was gifted in—working in the sports industry—into full-time ministry. I left everything I knew and the influence God had given me and began to pray into what He was showing me. The moment I began to take that stance in prayer, everything I prayed came to pass, because I was no longer just praying desires or what I thought God wanted for my life; but I was intent on pursuing what He truly had to say and then turning that back into prayer with Him.

MIDNIGHT PRAYERS

Have you ever heard of praying at midnight or ever done spiritual warfare at this time? If you haven't, then you truly have not carved out the level of authority God wants to bring you into. This is the time when the spiritual realm is easier to access, it's easier to hear God, and it's one of the best times to wage war against the enemy. This is the third and fourth watch. Right now, we're going to talk about the third watch, which is 12:00 a.m. to 3:00 a.m. This is when most warfare activity happens. The enemy, witches, warlocks, and satanists operate mostly around this time because they understand the spirit realm. How is it that most Christians never even attempt to pray at this time? I remember a word being spoken over some individuals and the Lord directed us to say, "Your victory is hailed at the midnight hour." We knew warfare was going to be associated with their victory, but it was going to take their pursuit in prayer at that time period. In the Scriptures, it says:

> *Immediately Jesus made the disciples get into the boat and go on ahead of him to the other side, while he dismissed the crowd. After he had dismissed them, he went up on a mountainside by himself to pray. Later that night, he was there alone, and the boat was already a considerable distance from land,*

buffeted by the waves because the wind was against it (Matthew 14:22-24 NIV).

Jesus spent most of the night alone on the mountain in prayer. There are mysteries of the mountaintop that we can understand from what Jesus did throughout the Scripture. During the fourth watch of the night, Jesus went out to them walking on the sea. When the disciples saw Him walking on the sea, they were terrified. "It's a ghost," they said, and cried out in fear. We see here that by evening Jesus was alone, spending time in prayer all the way up to 3:00 a.m. That is many, many hours in prayer by Himself, not corporately. This was the only way He was going to bypass the laws of gravity so they would not affect Him. If Jesus, being the Son of God, spent all night praying, then what is our excuse?

I'm not saying this has to be something that is done consistently because that is not realistic. But could you imagine what you could accomplish if once a year you engaged in a nine-hour prayer session? I remember the first time I was learning to press in with that type of duration. I remember when it was extremely hard to pray for just an hour. I grew in my prayer life and bypassed one hour to two hours, then to three hours, until one day we prayed from 9:00 p.m. until 6:00 a.m. for three days in a row. That was 27 hours of prayer, which is more time spent in prayer than most people accomplish in an entire year. What that prayer experience did for me is carve out a level and depth in the realm of the spirit that was unmatched by anything I had experienced before. The supernatural became alive. Angels begin to visit me, and I had many visitations of the Lord.

CHAPTER 8

INIQUITY HINDERS

Psalm 66:16-19 (NKJV) says:

Come and hear, all you who fear God, and I will declare what He has done for my soul. I cried to Him with my mouth, and He was extolled with my tongue. If I regard iniquity in my heart, the Lord will not hear. But certainly God has heard me; He has attended to the voice of my prayer.

We have to understand that iniquity is the driving force of rebellion and stubbornness in an individual's life. This will cause you to pray fleshly prayers. Iniquity is blinding, and that's why it's extremely important to renounce iniquity consistently. Make it a staple prayer throughout your whole life. You were born into iniquity and it can never leave you. The only thing you can do is keep it at bay, keep it under your feet by renouncing it and not allowing it to creep into your life.

You see, the systems of satan work like this. When satan is looking to attack your life, he looks for the easiest access point, which is iniquity. He knows that it will be so much easier to get you through iniquity in your bloodline than it would be to introduce something new. Iniquity is always the focal point of gaining access to someone's life because it's the easiest way. I consistently renounce iniquity daily or at least every other day to make sure that it's not trying to creep up and overtake me unawares. We see in this Psalm 66:18 (ESV): *"If I had cherished iniquity in my heart, the Lord would not have listened."* That is a dangerous thing, considering many people are driven by the force of iniquity in their bloodline. They create fleshly prayers, and then they wonder why God is not answering them. Are you entertaining iniquity unawares?

Repeat this prayer as often as you need to.

> I renounce all iniquity in my bloodline to four generations behind me in the name of Jesus.
>
> I renounce every claim of the enemy in my bloodline in the name of Jesus.

SEPARATION BRINGS THE ANOINTING

But now even more the report about him went abroad, and great crowds gathered to hear him and to be healed of their infirmities. But he would withdraw to desolate places and pray (Luke 5:15-16 ESV).

We see here that prayer is a powerful communication tool that was used between the individual and God. Although He spent time with His disciples in prayer and teaching them certain things, Jesus never neglected the fact that the source of His power and strength came from this interaction with God personally in those isolated and intimate places. The Scriptures say that before He chose His 12 disciples, Jesus went out to the mountain to pray, and He spent all night in prayer to God. When daylight came, He called His disciples to Him and chose 12 of them whom He designated as apostles.

How many times have you spent five or ten minutes in prayer and said, "God, this is too much; I need an answer"? How many times have you spent an hour in prayer and gotten frustrated that you didn't hear anything? How many times have you spent maybe an hour over a span of a few days and gotten frustrated because you didn't receive any instruction from heaven? The Scripture says that Jesus spent all night in prayer just to pick the 12 disciples. He knew the level of prayer required to make that decision. This choice would ultimately affect the world throughout all generations. Jesus knew that He must pray over that decision that night. It was no small task. Let this be a lesson to us to not get frustrated when we try to fit God into our time frame, demanding an answer when sometimes it requires duration in prayer to receive instruction.

Scripture also says, *"And in the morning rising up a great while before day."* Let's examine this phrase. *"Rising up a great while before day, he went out, and departed into a solitary place, and there prayed"* (Mark 1:35 KJV). We must understand that the day began in Israel around 4:30 a.m. Jesus would be in prayer three, four, five, or six hours before the day even started. Once He finished His communication with God, then He started the day. His disciples would be looking for Him, and then they would catch Him praying, and He would respond, "Let's go to this town or that town," and then He would do something spectacular! He walked up to a blind man and said, "What can I do for you?"

The blind man said, "I want to see."

Jesus said, "See!" and one fraction of a second later, his eyes opened. He would go to a leper and cleanse them; He would go to a person with a bad spirit and cast it out in a fraction of a second! A young boy was in a casket going to a funeral; He touched the coffin and said, "Live!" and the boy lived. What took Him fractions of a second with people had to take many hours in the morning with God. You see, the more time you spend with God, the less time you need to spend with people to see a miracle. The more time you spend in pursuit of God, He will reward you. Those who diligently seek Him are rewarded.

Our nature is to spend a minute in the morning with God and hours during the day trying to solve problems with mankind. The priority of Jesus was not ministry to people! That's our problem. You can't wait to heal the sick, cast out demons, raise the dead, or sing! You can have such zeal for these things that you neglect the very thing that will cause these things to happen. God wants you to spend time with Him first! Time in prayer is not wasted—it's time invested. Humankind's problems are only solved in His presence.

Another time, Jesus told His disciples to go to a town while He went to the mountain to pray. A man brought his boy with a demon to the disciples asking if they could cast it out, and they agreed. They began to work on this demon for hours. The Bible says Jesus came down from the mountain and said, "What's going on here?"

The man said, "I brought my son to Your disciples but they could not cast him out."

Jesus replied, "How long must I be with you?" It makes you wonder if Jesus was saying to Himself, "Have you not observed what I do in order to do these things? You see that I sneak away to pray to the Father for long durations. You see that I pull away to desolate places in the mountains many times to meet with God. Are you not seeing the template that I am laying out through My actions?"

We truly need to understand that walking with divine power and supernatural ability requires spending time in the presence of God. If we can discipline ourselves to press past the limitations our flesh places upon us and enter into a deep realm of the spirit, then the reality of heaven becomes our reality and anything inside the earth sphere will begin to listen to the authority we wield. What's really amazing and funny at the same time is that the Bible says the disciples waited until they were at dinner before they asked Jesus, in secret and quietly behind the walls, "Master, why couldn't we cast him out?" I bet they were pondering for a long time that day, thinking, *What in the world are we doing wrong?*

You see, many people are not willing to pay the price to truly carry the anointing. Anyone who walks in real power always has a deep intimacy and relationship with God. Those who carry real power are people who live life-styles of prayer and fasting—not just to get an answer or religiously doing it once a year. That accomplishes nothing when it comes to wielding authority in the spirit. You must have prepared yourself with God before you ever decide to go into public ministry. If not, the enemy will eat you alive. So many people have launched out prematurely because they taste a little bit of the supernatural or the giftings of the Spirit, and they immediately think that their time has come. They prematurely launch and get lit up by the enemy and backslide or never fully complete the assignment God gave them.

Spiritual Discernment

As believers we have to be very mindful of what we con-sider a move of God because there are many false prophets in the world, and more will continue to arise throughout the last days. The amount of deception will get worse and worse—so much so that the Bible says that if it were pos-sible, even the elect would be deceived. We are seeing a massive surge of false prophets in the prophetic movement.

These people are gifted but not consecrated. They use their gifting to extort God's people for money. You have to understand that the prophetic gifting opens the hearts of people. In 1 Corinthians 14:24-25 (NKJV) it says:

> *But if all prophesy, and an unbeliever or an uninformed person comes in, he is convinced by all, he is convicted by all. And thus the secrets of his heart are revealed; and so, falling down on his face, he will worship God and report that God is truly among you.*

The prophetic gift has the ability to unlock the heart and to lay thoughts bare before God, bringing people to repentance. This is why the prophetic is an extremely powerful tool, but it is also extremely dangerous in the wrong hands. This is why the Bible clearly warns us that many false prophets shall arise in the last days, deceiving many.

As the things of the spirit continue to infiltrate the earth and saturate it to a greater dimension because we are getting closer to the coming of the Lord, we begin to see the supernatural becoming evident everywhere we look. Secular people in the world are engaging in the occult, witchcraft activities, and are walking in deep realms of the spirit. One of the fastest-growing religions in the world is Wicca. What does this mean? This is a sign that there is much spiritual activity taking place and the majority of it is gross darkness. But when the world is at its darkest, this is when God is at His brightest. We must understand that we are to be a light in this world. Giftings are not a light. Giftings are an expression of the power of God, His sovereignty, and the supernatural. However, the problem is that most Christians live Hosea 4:6 (ISV): "*My people are destroyed because they lack knowledge.*" God did not say the heathen—He said "My people."

There are many Christians who have fallen as casualties of spiritual warfare because they lack knowledge in the things of the spirit. Most believers see a powerful gift and automatically validate the vessel as a holy man or a holy woman. Sometimes that can't be further from the truth! I have seen behind the curtain at the highest level in Christian circles and have been around people with the most tremendous prophetic ability, but their character was in shambles. These leaders are committing adultery, having multiple affairs. They pimp God's people for money. Many of them function in witchcraft because of extreme narcissism. We have to be very careful that we do not let what we see as a powerful gift make us think that they must be right with God. Jesus Himself said very clearly, *"You will know them by their fruits"* (Matthew 7:16 NKJV).

A person can have a very strong gifting but give off no sense of presence at all. That may sound contradictory, but it's not, and I'm going to explain why. There is a difference between presence and a demonstration of power. When someone carries true presence, there is a tangible, holy manifestation within the atmosphere, and these people glow with God's glory and light. You can physically see their eyes glowing with light. In Matthew 6:22, it says that your eye is like a lamp that provides light for your whole body. When your eye is healthy or good, your whole body will be full of light. But if your eyes are unhealthy, your whole body is filled with darkness. And if the light you think you have is actually darkness, how deep that darkness is!

When someone truly carries presence, they are a reflector of what they behold. The Bible says, *"As in water face reflects face, so a man's heart reveals the man"* (Proverbs 27:19 NKJV). You are what you behold. The Bible says that if I behold Him then I am changed into His image from glory to glory (see 2 Corinthians 3:18). We, as the church, have lost the art of beholding.

You may say, "OK, Joshua, can you break that down into layman's terms?" We must get back to the simplicity of the gospel. We must get back to the simplicity of coming to God like a little child. Procedures, protocols, and traditions are blockades to actually obtaining the presence of God. When you learn to practice surrender and you do this on a daily basis, the Holy Spirit begins to move in your life stronger and stronger. The more you surrender, the more of Him you take in, because you will be able to behold Him in the spirit. There have been many times when my prayer consisted of nothing but looking at Him. You may be saying to yourself, *How in the world do you do that when you don't see anything?* That's a good question. When I first started doing this, I didn't see anything, but I felt the proximity; I felt the closeness. I have felt the ability to connect to Him at a deeper level because I started to turn the eyes of my heart toward Him. This can only be practiced. There is no amount of reading, studying, or listening to teaching that will be able to teach you how to do this until you start putting it into action and walking it out for yourself.

As I started spending time in His presence beholding Him, I began to see Him. The more I would look at Him, the clearer He would become. He is an ever-present help in times of trouble. He is right there! You just have to know how to access Him. I sit down in a chair and start to pray in the spirit. As I'm surrendering in prayer, I begin to focus my heart to look at Him. Sometimes I don't even pray; I just focus and stare within my heart to access Him. When I do that, visitations explode. God visits me in the middle of the night. I'll be lying in bed and the room gets extremely bright and He walks in and just stares at me. I can feel it all around me.

This is called practicing His presence. This is not functioning in a spiritual gift in order to manipulate an encounter. This is why demonstrations of the Spirit must always be blended with true presence before you ever label a man or woman of God as holy. In the body of Christ, we're seeing too many very defiled and unconsecrated people operating in a gift without a measure of holiness.

Let's break down a little bit of what I was saying about fasting so that you get a clearer understanding. Remember, fasting is a spiritual principle, a law that God has established within the earth. Anyone can open that door and enter the realm of the spirit and obtain power, whether good or bad. There is a thin line between the natural and the supernatural. As I mentioned before, many people in the occult, practicing witchcraft, or satanists understand that they must crucify the body and pay a price in order to obtain spiritual power. There are many people out there on platforms who understand that they can fast and tap into the realm of the spirit and easily manipulate people who are not sharp in their discernment. The Scriptures say:

> *Then Jesus was led up by the Spirit into the wilderness to be tempted by the devil. And when He had fasted forty days and forty nights, afterward He was hungry. Now when the tempter came to Him, he said, "If You are the Son of God, command that these stones become bread."*

> *But He answered and said, "It is written, 'Man shall not live by bread alone, but by every word that proceeds from the mouth of God.'"*

> *Then the devil took Him up into the holy city, set Him on the pinnacle of the temple, and said to Him, "If You are the Son of God, throw Yourself down. For it is written: 'He shall give His angels charge over you,' and, 'In their hands they shall bear you up, lest you dash your foot against a stone.'"*

> *Jesus said to him, "It is written again, 'You shall not tempt the Lord your God.'"*

> *Again, the devil took Him up on an exceedingly high mountain, and showed Him all the kingdoms of the world and their glory. And he said to Him, "All these things I will give You if You will fall down and worship me."*

Then Jesus said to him, "Away with you, Satan! For it is written, 'You shall worship the Lord your God, and Him only you shall serve.'"

Then the devil left Him, and behold, angels came and ministered to Him (Matthew 4:1-11 NKJV).

Let's break down these scriptures to see that the temptations Jesus faced are the same temptations we all face when we are in the pursuit of God. The first temptation was satan coming to Jesus and challenging Him to turn stones into bread. Jesus responded to him saying, *"Man shall not live on bread alone but on every word that comes from the mouth of God."* You need to recognize by that statement that you do not survive on physical food alone. Yes, physical food keeps your natural body alive, but how many people are walking around like zombies? They may be completely nourished with physical food and look nice in the natural, but in reality they are like dead people walking because there is no Word within them. The Word is truly what you feast upon. The Word is what you live by.

I heard one of the most shocking statements recently, and it really showed the condition of the church. There was a study done on specific topics that people wanted to engage with and learn about in the church, and the Word of God was the last on the list. The least focused-upon topic, the least engaging topic, and the least exciting topic in the body of Christ was the Word of God. The topics on the top of that list were the supernatural, the prophetic, God's power, and everything you can think of in between, but nobody wanted the Word. Nobody wanted to learn the Word. Do you know how dangerous that is? That is the most dangerous thing the body of Christ could ever face—people who are engaged in spiritual activities and functioning in the spirit realm with absolutely no foundation in the Word.

This is how the great deception is coming in. This is how believers are deceived day by day, and it's getting worse until the coming of Christ. People truly do not know the Word of God. They care more about the expression. They care more about signs and wonders. They care more about revival than they do getting the foundation for all of this to actually take place. They're putting the cart before the horse. Do you know a lot of believers have made revival an idol? Do you know a lot of believers have made signs and wonders their idol? It's the truth. Maybe you are one of them and the Holy Spirit is beginning to convict you right now. That's OK. Repeat this prayer of repentance.

PRAYER OF ACTIVATION AND DELIVERANCE

> Father, in the name of Jesus, I repent for all idolatry, in Jesus' name.
>
> I repent for making the expression of Your power an idol in my life.
>
> I repent for making signs and wonders and revivals an idol in my life, in the name of Jesus.

> Restore me, because I know once I have proper alignment in Your Word, all of these things will begin to take place.
>
> Signs and wonders will follow me; the blessing will pursue me and overtake me.
>
> Revival will break forth within me that can spread to others!

If there is no Word of God within your spirit, if you're not getting downloads from Him consistently, then you truly are spiritually malnourished. Jesus said it clearly, *"Man shall not live by bread alone, but by every word that proceeds from the mouth of God"* (Matthew 4:4 NKJV). I know that my nourishment, my substance, and everything I need to move forward is found in His Word.

A close friend of mine recently had a very disturbing vision. They saw all of these believers in a drive-thru line at a restaurant. When they pulled up to the place to order, they were ordering spiritual gifts. As they were ordering their spiritual gifts, just like they ask you if you would like a side of fries with that, the person on the microphone asked each and every person, "Would you like the Holy Spirit with that?"

Each person said, "No, I don't want that—that's too hard of a price to pay. We just want the gifts." They didn't realize that Jesus was sitting on the other side watching each and every person go through, and He was disappointed because they didn't want the Lord. They didn't want His Spirit. They didn't want to have to walk the life of a Christian—they just wanted the giftings. We are literally seeing that in this present hour now more than ever.

DO NOT TEST THE LORD

Let's examine the second temptation that Jesus experienced and that you will experience in your pursuit.

> *Then the devil took him to the holy city and had him stand on the highest point of the temple. "If you are the Son of God," he said, "throw yourself down. For it is written: 'He will command his angels concerning you, and they will lift you up in their hands, so that you will not strike your foot against a stone.'" Jesus answered him, "It is also written: 'Do not put the Lord your God to the test'"* (Matthew 4:5-7 NIV).

First, we need to understand that these encounters were taking place in the realm of the spirit. In this temptation we see that the devil took Him to the holy city and had Him stand on the highest point of the temple. Why? The holy city carries an atmosphere, just like a church, your life, and any place where God's presence resides. The atmosphere is a real thing. The reason the devil took Jesus to the holy city is because the atmosphere was so strong. You know when you're in an atmosphere of God's presence at church and it's so strong that you feel that you can do anything and that God could use you to do anything? That is the atmosphere I'm talking about. That is why satan took Him to the holy city.

The second portion of this temptation says that satan brought Jesus to the highest point of the temple, which represented the most extreme flow of presence and power that

He could be experiencing in the moment that temptation was happening. This is why satan said, *"If you are the Son of God."* He was testing the sovereignty of Jesus here. He was testing His identity. He brought Him to a place where He experienced more power and presence than any human in the history of the world.

Imagine what Jesus was feeling in this moment! This is why satan began to test His identity and who He really was and placed Him in a position where He felt the strongest. He placed Him in a position where God's power and presence was like no other. Now you see where the temptation came in—he wanted to test Jesus in His strength and in a place where He felt God's power and presence so much that anything was possible. The enemy twisted the Scriptures referencing God's protection in that moment to see if he would get a response from Jesus. But we see that Jesus answered him and said, *"It is also written: 'Do not put the Lord your God to the test.'"*

So let's break this down for a second. We must understand that God does protect, God does give His angels charge over you, but this is not a license to go and do things outside of wisdom. This is not a license to go and put God to the test just because He says angels are there for you. If you jump out of a plane with no parachute, you will enter heaven early. You can't go up in a plane and say, "Well, angels are going to help me." Is it possible? Has it happened that people have fallen out of a plane and survived? Yes. But that doesn't mean you can jump from a plane and expect to live. That is testing God. You believe God protects you but you still lock your doors at night, right? I believe God can protect me, but I still put on my seat belt. We have to understand that one of the temptations satan brings to people is he places them in a position in which they feel invincible or they're experiencing God's power and presence and they fall for the trap.

The enemy is constantly testing your identity. He is constantly throwing out, "Well, if God said this, then ABC and so forth." This is why we never respond outside of the wisdom and Spirit of God. The number-one problem in the world, not just believers but for people in general, is lack of identity. They truly do not know what they were created to do or what God has called them to do.

Speaking from a believer's perspective, we understand that God has called us to something great. He is constantly reaffirming His Word and His promises through people, dreams and visions, and impressions of His Word. We are constantly wondering how we get to that place of fulfillment. You can see why the devil targets this area more than anything else. If he can get you to question your identity, then he has won because he can always manipulate how he wants you to see yourself.

Throughout Scripture, God is constantly reminding us of who we are in Christ and how He sees us because this is one of the main attack points of the enemy. This is more and more rampant, particularly with the current gender identity issues. Satan is twisting the truth so far to even make people think they are different genders. The level of mental anguish and attack in this generation is extremely concerning. Again, understanding the Bible, there is nothing we can do to stop what is coming to the earth and where things are heading into the coming of the Lord. But take comfort knowing that even as darkness increases, God's glory and light also increases. The Bible says, *"He who endures to the end shall be saved"* (Mark 13:13 NKJV). We need the ability to endure against persecution and what is coming to the body of Christ. We are starting to become the outcast, the hated, and the minority in religion and spirituality. Why? Because the name of Jesus brings conviction and offense to those who have rejected Him.

As I prayed, God began to show me through multiple supernatural encounters that what was coming could not be prayed away. I recently had three visitations in which I heard the Father speak from heaven. As I began to see chaos happening in the earth, I started to run to the mountain to pray, and then I heard God speak from heaven, saying, "You cannot pray this away." I immediately knew that I had to turn to the people of the world and cry out, "Repent and renounce your sin—it is the only thing that will protect you!"

As I was screaming to the world and weeping as people began to renounce their sin, a spiritual bubble came over them and I immediately knew what it was. The Bible says, *"But as the days of Noah were, so also will the coming of the Son of Man be"* (Matthew 24:37 NKJV). I knew that this repentance and renouncing of sin was actually a spiritual ark of protection over the people. Just as the physical ark protected Noah and his family from God's judgment, so shall the spiritual ark of repenting and renouncing protect people from God's coming judgment. I'll never forget in this moment hearing in the heavens all around me, "God's judgment fire is upon the earth."

As I got on my knees in that moment, I recognized that as I saw judgment fire sweep through the earth like a tsunami, I was protected because I was on my knees. Let this be a sign to us all. Come back to a place of repentance. Come back to a place of humility. Come back to a place of renouncing your sin consistently. The Bible says, "*Bear fruit in keeping with repentance*" (Matthew 3:8 ESV). Walk out your salvation with fear and trembling. God is for you. God is with you. He will deliver you and protect you, no matter what is to befall the earth. When we place ourselves in alignment with His will and with His plans, He will pour out His spirit in such measure that nothing will be able to prevent the plans that He has for your life.

Worship God Only

In Luke 4:5-8 (NKJV), we read about the third temptation that Jesus faced.

> *Then the devil, taking Him up on a high mountain, showed Him all the kingdoms of the world in a moment of time. And the devil said to Him, "All this authority I will give You, and their glory; for this has been delivered to me, and I give it to whomever I wish. Therefore, if You will worship before me, all will be Yours." And Jesus answered and said to him, "Get behind Me, Satan! For it is written,*

'You shall worship the Lord your God, and
Him only you shall serve.'"

This example shows that one of the most common temptations that satan brings to mankind is the need for power,
the need for recognition, and the desire for control. Satan
spoke from this perspective to try to tempt Jesus because
he used this concept in the Garden of Eden. When satan
approached Eve in the Garden, he said to her, "*God knows
that if you eat the fruit from that tree, you will learn about good
and evil and you will be like God!*" (Genesis 3:5 NCV). Satan
was speaking of exercising a dimension of authority through
knowledge that they were not privy to. Satan craftily told
them, "You will not die but you will become like God." I
believe he spoke to them from this perspective because of his
own fall. His selfish pride and cravings for power and authority cost him his place in heaven. He recognized the pull of
this temptation because it was within him.

This is why God wants us to yield to His authority and
knowledge. He knows what is best for us. When we do not
follow in the steps of humility, satan has a grasp and foot-
hold to try to take us into the destruction of pride.

Eve started the conversation with, "We may eat of the
fruit of the trees in the garden." The serpent then said to
her, "*You will not surely die. For God knows that in the day
you eat of it your eyes will be opened, and you will be like God,
knowing good and evil.*" This exchange highlights humani-
ty's desire to be a god in their own eyes when the flesh is
activated. During the temptation of Christ, satan offered
all the kingdoms of the world to Jesus if He would only bow

down and worship him. This experience was not uncommon to Jesus. The enemy comes to any individual who will give him a place with that same offer.

In our culture, we see this in many arenas. Celebrities and the wealthy often state that they had to make a deal with the devil in order to carry the influence, fame, and power that they have. They say that they have sold their soul, not realizing that no one can actually sell their soul to anyone. Satan creates this illusion to convince the individual that they are unredeemable because of an act of disobedience to gain power. Satan usually requires blood in order to make a pact or some sort of blood covenant exchange to give the power and influence to that individual.

Scripture tells us that there is a price to pay for every soul. Jesus overcame and won the victory over death, hell, and the grave for all humankind! Christ has already bought us back with His blood and given us eternal life through grace. Anyone who says they have sold their soul to satan is living in deception because our souls were already purchased by Christ. Their soul is literally paid for in full and not for sale!

This is why satan is constantly targeting identity. We must begin to meditate on who God says we are and what His thoughts are toward our life. This will place within us the very faith to resist the devil when he comes knocking with false realities, false ideologies, and false perceptions of who we are. Repeat this prayer.

Prayer of Activation and Deliverance

Father, in the name of Jesus, every lie of the enemy about who I am and who You called me to be I flush it out by the fire of the Holy Spirit right now, in the name of Jesus.

Father, I believe who You say You are. You are not a God to lie. All Your promises are yes and amen.

I choose to believe the report of the Lord. Every lie, every manipulation, and every deception that has been fashioned against my life, against my mind, and against my identity, I destroy it by the fire of the Holy Spirit, in the name of Jesus.

Father, help me to know Your will. Help me to know what You have called me to do by Your Spirit, in Jesus' name.

CHAPTER 9

THE MARINE KINGDOM

There is a lot of activity that is spoken about in the Bible when it comes to the ocean and rivers and bodies of water. There are certain gods referenced throughout Scripture that a modern-day reader may not understand. Ancient people served certain gods in various regions, often gods who were tied to that region due to the landscape of the area as well as the cultural response to that particular landform. We also read examples of sea monsters, Leviathan, and dragons, particularly in the book of Revelation.

Revelation 12:13 (ESV) says, "*And when the dragon saw that he had been thrown down to the earth, he pursued the woman who had given birth to the male child.*" This is an attack against mankind. This shows a type and shadow of Mary giving birth to Jesus, and it says there was an attack or that the dragon pursued the woman who had given birth to the male child. The woman was given two wings of a great eagle to fly from the presence of the serpent to her place in the wilderness where she was nourished for a time and times and half a time. Revelation 12:15 (ESV) says, "*The serpent poured water like a river out of his mouth after the woman, to sweep her away with a flood.*"

"*To sweep her away with a flood*"—let's take a look at this phrase from a spiritual standpoint. The attacks being released by the devil originate from the marine kingdom. The Scripture describes this occurrence in detail, "*water like a river out of his mouth,*" but the earth helped the woman in Revelation 12:16 (ESV): "*But the earth came to the help of the woman, and the earth opened its mouth and swallowed the river that the dragon had poured from his mouth.*"

The book of Revelation helps us have a greater understanding of the various types of spiritual warfare we encounter as believers. We have to understand that certain regions of the earth have been dedicated to the spirits operating in that region—in this example, to the spirits of the water. In Revelation 12, John explained that the devil/dragon opened its mouth to swallow up the woman by a river and poured out water from its mouth. The marine kingdom operates in water. This is an example of satan working in the marine kingdom to try and overthrow the woman by the force of water. There are spiritual attacks that derive directly from the marine kingdom.

In the demonic realm, people who think they are selling their soul to the devil are convinced that they are exchanging their own soul to gain power or influence. Your soul literally cannot be sold. But people will fall into this deception, believing that they are handing over something they don't own to gain what they desire—be it power, wealth, status, or influence. This deception occurs with a particular type of spirit. These spiritual contracts, agreements, and transactions are done in the marine kingdom through water. Covenants are made for finances in the marine kingdom. Covenants are made for wealth and influence in the marine kingdom. The marine kingdom operates in the ocean or in that realm. If you physically went down into the ocean, I don't think you will see it. You are not physically engaging in the spirit realm in the physical ocean or water.

While they do not operate from the physical ocean, marine spirits have control of the regions around oceans, waterways, and rivers. Marine spirits are the ones that give people fame through their demonic realm. Marine spirits give wealth and influence. Think about this—it is not a coincidence that you throw a penny into a fountain and make a wish! In reality, you are actually aligning yourself with the marine kingdom through the offering of money. Finances are strongly associated with the marine kingdom. It is not a happenstance cultural tradition to use wishing wells. Have you ever stopped to consider why people started throwing money into a well with water instead of into trees or the woods or off a cliff? Look at it from a spiritual perspective—why is it that money was to be attached to water in order to bring about a wish or desire? It's the marine kingdom in operation.

If you take a moment to consider our culture through the years, it helps to shed light on what is going on and the spirit operating behind much of our culture. Let's just examine the music industry. When it comes to music videos in this day and age, I don't watch them at all. But back in the day when MTV first started with music videos on television, the essence of the marine kingdom was extremely evident. The marine kingdom consists of and always associates with perversion, lust, seduction, and influence. Many of the artists who are or have been at the top of the music industry have "made a deal with the devil" and completely succumbed to the marine kingdom.

Fame, finances, influence, and even technology are huge assets utilized by marine spirits. However, you can always see the imprint of satan's hand. He is deceptive but also full of pride and wants to be recognized. He will show his involvement and will clearly leave his mark. I remember years ago, Ricky Martin had a very popular song called "She Bangs." In the music video, he is seen many times underwater and under the ocean, singing and dancing with demonic spirits. This is a clear depiction of how people enter the marine kingdom through the enticement of these spirits. There are so many artists who show themselves under the water or who have videos or album covers showing themselves in the lost city of Atlantis. This is a prime example of the marine kingdom at work.

Prayer of Deliverance and Activation

I cancel every negative effect of the marine kingdom working against my life, working against my family, working against my finances, working against my children, in Jesus' mighty name.

I break the hold of the marine kingdom off my household.

I break the hold of marine powers off my spouse.

I break the hold of marine powers off my mind.

God, flush out any influence of the marine kingdom from my mind, in Jesus' name.

I declare that God is delivering my mind from bombarding thoughts, in Jesus' mighty name.

I renounce every claim of the marine kingdom over my life on behalf of me and my spouse, in Jesus' name.

I reject every ring that was placed upon me or placed upon my spouse from under the water in the name of Jesus.

I renounce every ungodly soul tie, in Jesus' name.

I renounce every bill of marriage and every contract that has my name on it from under the water. It is burned by fire right now, in the name of Jesus.

Father, deliver me from the powers of every water dragon, in the name of Jesus.

Deliver me from the powers of water serpents, in the name of Jesus.

ENTRY POINTS FOR THE MARINE KINGDOM

Marine spirits will always target families, households, and children. They look for initiation through access points. Some people are more vulnerable or susceptible than others due to their actual geographical location. If you look at coastlines, often you can identify a pattern or tendency for different levels of perversion. A high level of child trafficking is associated with coastlines of most nations. That's the power of the marine kingdom.

Many times, the highest level of perversion in a state or region will be at the coast. For example, look at the cities of Miami, Daytona Beach, or San Francisco. Marine spirits are not in high operation in a more wooded area or mountainous region such as Montana or maybe Arizona. These wooded areas would operate more under the principality correlated to nature for that region, like Wicca/witchcraft. Marine spirits typically will not have a stronghold in a heavily wooded or mountainous area. Different spirits operate and have strongholds in different regions. For example, in Redding, California, the redwood forest there has trees that are the size of Volkswagens. They are so large that they are 10 to 15 feet wide—just huge trees. There is a large activity within the hippie movement, witches, and Wicca in that region, with the strength of the spirits operating in that area stemming from some idol worship of the trees and access of the Wicca spirits in that area.

Marine spirits have a large influence in the coastlines of Africa, in the Caribbean, and the Bermuda Triangle. Now when you look at the activity involved within the Bermuda triangle, it's a very loose analysis, not something that is a definitive. I have not been taken there in the spirit yet, so I don't know definitely about that in the spirit. When I share about being taken in the spirit, God actually takes me there in reality. This experience is total reality but you are in the spirit realm. You are, without a shadow of a doubt, experiencing reality. Even if the activity that occurs is wild and outside of anything you have ever experienced, you have the ability to interpret what it means.

The book of Ezekiel is an example of a supernatural experience. Ezekiel was taken in the spirit and began to see crazy and wild things happening in the temple. But what he saw was the reality of what was actually taking place in the spirit. So when I say I've not been taken to the marine kingdom yet, I've experienced a portion of it. I've gone down to the ocean before and seen certain things, but I am believing God that He'll take me behind the scenes down there. I'm believing that He will show me things in the marine kingdom to better understand it.

God has shown me many things in the spirit. I've seen God. I've been to hell twice. In one of those experiences, I was in a meeting that was crazy. I was in hell in an amphitheater. In that amphitheater, satan was teaching and I was sitting there looking around, thinking, *All these meetings of these wicked people.* I thought to myself, *Oh my gosh, they don't know I'm here.* Because I spoke it out loud and within my heart, they all turned and looked at me. They could hear me. Then satan was down at the bottom and he lifted his hand and billions of rats started taking off running at me and then boom! I was out of there! Rats represent poverty and they represent an attack on finances. So those animals in the spirit symbolize bringing harm and hindrance financially because of where the gospel is going to go through this ministry.

There are many things that happen or occur in the natural realm that are so wild that they cannot be explained. We must understand that the spirit realm is just as real, if not more so, than the natural realm we experience. The strengthening of the marine kingdom occurs in natural regions where there is an opening or leaning toward those doors being opened. For example, there is a lot of mystery surrounding the Bermuda Triangle, but there is certainly the possibility of the marine kingdom operating in that region. One thing to recognize in the marine kingdom and in the way satan operates is that he uses symbols to signal his work and to perform rituals. The triangle is one of those symbols. Triangles can operate as a door for the enemy in the spirit world. Look at the pentagram, the all-seeing eye on the US dollar bill, the pyramids of Egypt—they can all be used as a doorway for satan or as a part of satanic rituals.

PRIDE AND REBELLION

Son of man, say to the prince of Tyre, Thus says the Lord God: Because your heart is lifted up and you have said and thought, I am a god, I sit in the seat of the gods, in the heart of the seas (Ezekiel 28:2 AMPC).

This Scripture says that this person or entity is exalting himself. This passage highlights that these gods are associated with the sea and with water.

Speak, and say, Thus saith the Lord God; Behold, I am against thee, Pharaoh king of Egypt, the great dragon that lieth in the midst of his rivers, which hath said, My river is mine own, and I have made it for myself (Ezekiel 29:3 KJV).

Yet you are a man, and not a god, though you set your heart as the heart of a god (Ezekiel 28:2 NKJV).

Look at the resistance of this marine spirit. This is a dangerous monster. This spirit says, "I am a god, I sit in the seats of God in the midst of the seas." It is evident in this verse that this spiritual entity is being strengthened from marine spirits and from marine powers. One sign or evidence that marine spirits are at work is a high level of pride. Marine spirits operate in strong rebellion and resistance from a deep-rooted place of pride. This is one reason why marine spirits only go out by prayer and fasting. When you are under attack or under the influence of the marine kingdom, deliverance from this type of attack will only come through prayer and fasting. Fasting is essential for this deliverance.

Along with pride and rebellion, when you find marine spirits or the marine kingdom in operation, there will be high-level sexual perversion. For example, in South Korea, there is a whole park that celebrates and exalts male genitalia. There are male private parts in statue form all over the park. People from around the world travel to South Korea to this tourist attraction that celebrates sexuality and prosperity through male private parts as statues and art. Water spirits in the marine kingdom are associated with both of these things. The people instilled a covenant with the water spirits. Tourists from all over the world come and offer this kind of sacrifice to the sea. This is the working of the marine kingdom.

THE DRAGON

Let's take a look at sea monsters and dragons and how they operate within the marine kingdom. Psalm 74:13-14 (KJV) says, "*Thou didst divide the sea by thy strength: thou brakest the heads of the dragons in the waters. Thou brakest the heads of leviathan in pieces, and gavest him to be meat to the people inhabiting the wilderness.*" The word for *sea monster* is *tannin*. It literally means "dragon, sea monster, serpent, sea or river monster." It is really focused around the aspect of a marine spirit and marine dragon.

Another scripture that deals with this same perspective is: "*Thou shalt tread upon the lion and adder: the young lion and the dragon shalt thou trample under feet*" (Psalm 91:13 KJV). This is talking about a sea monster, using the same word, *tannin*, for "monster, dragon, serpent under the water, sea or river monster." So every time dragons are mentioned in Scripture, think of: "*In that day the Lord with his sore and great and strong sword shall punish leviathan the piercing serpent, even leviathan that crooked serpent; and he shall slay the dragon that is in the sea*" (Isaiah 27:1 KJV). A lot of these scriptures emphasize dealing with sea serpents, sea monsters, and dragons—things that are really spiritual. God has given us the authority to have dominion over anything that satan can throw at us as believers.

MARINE RITUALS

Now let's examine the various manifestations of water spirits, what they do, and how they actually function. There are many ways that people invoke the power of water spirits through worship. One of the ways people worship is performing rituals on beach fronts or going into the water. In many African nations, certain religious sects engage in worship by spending days in prayer in the sea. Often, they will wear white gowns and burn candles as part of their rituals. The wearing of white gowns is often used in witchcraft and ritualistic worship. This can be found in Lagos, Nigeria, which has a very strong area of demonic activity.

People also bathe in ponds or rivers at certain times of the day such as midnight or midday, which is interesting because the Bible references these same specific time periods. Psalm 91:6 (NIV) says, "*the plague that destroys at midday.*" Often, we read in Scripture about spiritual activity or rituals such as baptism into water set to be performed at midnight. Another part of spirit worship is to offer objects to the spirit in exchange for power, wealth, or influence. People will throw objects like clothes, jewelry, underwear, beads, chickens, or goats directly into the water under the direction of a priest or priestess to appease the water spirits in those areas. Another way to invoke the water spirits is by sprinkling "holy water" or purification rituals involving the washing of hands or feet in sacred streams or rivers.

Part of these rituals involve priests taking young girls to rivers to "marry" them to the river spirits. These girls usually become prostitutes and lesbians and find it extremely difficult to marry or keep their marriage. One ritual is to offer a newborn baby to the water spirits. A new baby is dropped into the river on the day of birth and collected seven days later. If the baby dies, that means he was unacceptable to the river gods. But if the baby survives, the gods have accepted him or her. This is actually a dedication of the baby to the water spirits. Many of the sects who worship water spirits wearing the white garments will usually build their churches near rivers, deriving from these powers.

Many coastal area fishermen also make sacrifices to these spirits. In Haiti, there is a waterfall where voodoo priestess from all over the world will come annually to offer worship to the water spirits to receive greater voodoo power. The people will manifest river spirits. They make covenant tokens with water spirits. In many areas of the world, people will form covenants with the water spirits and draw power from them through water spirit idol worship.

Fountains are created and people are asked to drop coins into the fountains to make a wish. But this is actually water spirit worship! These coins are covenant tokens, making a covenant with water spirits. In Venice, California, there is a beachfront that sees a lot of occult activity. It is like a market or exhibition center of satan where virtually every occult group is represented, marketing their spiritual wares, their spiritual objects right in that city in California near the coast.

Another form or manifestation of water spirit worship is the restriction of fishing on certain days or during certain seasons. They do this in order to appease the spirits. In Nigeria, tens of thousands of people come to worship a river goddess there. Many of the kings and presidents of various nations go to raise altars at the source of rivers to draw strength from water spirits to secure power. Some African presidents are known to have raised such altars at the source of the Nile River. Just as it was mentioned in Scripture that the dragon called the river his own, they erect altars to the marine spirits that operate in that region. Another example of this type of worship occurs at the full moon every November in Thailand. The local fishermen and village people will decorate their boats with flowers. They say that the troubles of the people will float downstream during this sacred festival. They are expected to worship at the river when they decorate the boats and come to the river at full moon.

Let's take a look at another part of the marine kingdom from Scripture. In the Old Testament, there is a story about a Philistine god named Dagon. Dagon was a god or idol worshiped by the Philistines that was associated with a water spirit. In 1 Samuel 5:1-5 (NIV), it says:

> *After the Philistines had captured the ark of God, they took it from Ebenezer to Ashdod. Then they carried the ark into Dagon's temple and set it beside Dagon. When the people of Ashdod rose early the next day, there was Dagon, fallen on his face on the ground before the ark of the Lord! They took Dagon and put him back in his place. But the following morning when they rose, there was Dagon, fallen on his face on the ground before the ark of the Lord! His head and hands had been broken off and were lying on the threshold; only his body remained. That is why to this day neither the priests of Dagon nor any others who enter Dagon's temple at Ashdod step on the threshold.*

Dagon was chief deity for the Philistine people, and the worship of this pagan god dates back to the third millennium. According to ancient mythology, he was a fish god represented as half man and half fish. Dagon is also actually part of the story of Jonah as well. The Assyrians in Nineveh, to whom Jonah was sent as a missionary, worshiped Dagon. Jonah did not go straight to Nineveh but was transported there miraculously by a great fish, which had great meaning for the Ninevites. When Jonah finally arrived in Nineveh, he made quite an appearance and impression on the people. Jonah was a man who had been inside this great fish for three days and was directly deposited by that fish on dry land unscathed. The Ninevites, who primarily worshiped a deity that was half fish, half man, had to be impressed by this incredible event. It grabbed their attention and brought them to a place of repentance. It is incredible that God, in His sovereignty and mercy, used such an object (the whale or great fish) that was obviously used in their own idol worship to deliver His chosen prophet to declare the good news and bring repentance to a people!

DREAM IMAGERY

When dealing with the marine kingdom, your dream life is vitally important. There are many indicators in the dream life that you are dealing with the marine kingdom or attacks from marine spirits. Whenever you dream of alligators, this is a sign of the leviathan spirit attacking you in your dream life. Leviathan represents pride. Pride is strongly represented in marine spirit attacks and is highly resistant to the things of God. Alligators have scales that are very strong, like armor. When we read about the leviathan in the Bible in the book of Job, it describes leviathan as being a piercing serpent and that its armor is so interwoven together that air cannot even get through it. The scales serve as a shield.

Scripture says no man can tame the leviathan. The spirit of leviathan operates in pride, so it is impossible to be delivered from leviathan alone. You can't say, "Well, I delivered myself from leviathan." That's pride. You cannot be delivered from pride by being prideful. The only thing that leviathan responds to is humility. The kingdom of God operates in the opposite spirit to the marine kingdom or the kingdom of the enemy. The only way to defeat pride and/or leviathan spirit is to embrace a spirit of humility. So if you are experiencing dreams that involve alligators, indicating the leviathan spirit, you need to recognize that you are operating somewhere in pride. The way to overcome this attack is to humble yourself, get on your knees, pray, renounce, and repent of any pride and stubbornness in your heart and life. Allow God to soften your heart. The Bible says that if you draw near to God, He will draw near to you. Seek His face from a repentant and humble heart, and you will be set free from these types of attacks from the marine kingdom.

The size of the alligator or animal is also indicative of the power of that spirit coming against you. I had a dream a long time ago in which a massive alligator the size of a human attacked a particular person, and literally the enemy took them out. So take that into consideration when dealing with these attacks as well. If you dream of a small alligator, it still needs to be dealt with by prayer and humility. If it is a larger alligator, prayer and fasting is the way to address it and be set free.

Remember that if you see snakes or scorpions or any dangerous animals in your dreams, those are representative of an attack coming against you in the spirit. You associate the level of attack with the danger of the animal in the natural. If you get bit by a rattlesnake, it can literally kill you. So if you get bit by rattlesnake in your dream, that is an indication of a heavy spiritual attack. If you get bit by a king cobra or black mamba, the most deadly snakes in the world, this is a serious attack that will require days of fasting and prayer and seeking God to dissolve the atmosphere that was released against you.

Other ways to identify spiritual attacks in your dreams is when you experience a dream involving dirty water or dealing with frogs. This is representative of an unclean spirit. Frogs in the natural look very harmless, but if you look at their face, they look like the most demonic creature in the world. They are similar to snakes, which are wicked looking in the natural. In the book of Revelation unclean spirits come out like toads or frogs. This represents a level of perversion, filth, and uncleanliness. There are some frogs that are extremely dangerous in the natural. There are some tree frogs that excrete toxins that people will lick to experience a euphoric or psychedelic phenomenon. This is actually a supernatural projection where they are having interactions with demonic entities while under the influence of this toxin. This is mentioned in Revelation, and it makes me wonder if the increase of these frogs in the Amazon is related to people seeking out these encounters. This could usher in a mentality of delusion at the coming of the antichrist. It is going to take strong delusion and deception and strong resistance in the mind for people to resist the very nature of God. These types of hallucinogens are really gateways to contracts or covenants in the spirit world under the water.

Another type of covenant can occur with spiritual mermaids entering people. You may have had dreams of mermaids, which function from a place of seduction. They use certain makeup and hairstyles and project seduction from the eyes. I can look at someone's eyes and within two seconds, I can see marine kingdom water on their eyes. They have a different glaze. There is a specific look of seduction from the marine kingdom. The Bible warns against the seduction in the eyes in the book of Proverbs. Proverbs also mentions a woman releasing demonic power through the eyes to capture people. There is a power that operates from the marine kingdom that is meant to attract people, to capture their attention, and to put them under their spell so to speak.

It is so important to use discernment when dealing with these mermaid or siren-type spirits. It is best to not engage with that person by looking them in the eyes unless you are seasoned in dealing with them. These spirits will use the eyes to try to seduce and bring people into captivity. I've done deliverances and been in pulpits and when I prayed for people, I saw that spirit in a lot of the people's eyes. I immediately saw their thoughts or knew what they were doing. Even when praying for them, sometimes I kept my head down and focused because as I prayed for their deliverance, that spirit tried to look for a way of entrance.

When people are beginning to renounce marine and mermaid spirits, they will go into dreams and fight mermaids and kill them in their dreams after a time of deliverance. Their testimony is usually something along the lines of, "Oh my, I can't believe this just happened!" This is just evidence that the deliverance is taking place. Another thing you need to be aware of is accepting any type of ring in a dream because it could be a spirit "husband" or "wife" trying to marry you in the spirit. This can be a spirit trying to block you from marriage or attacking your current marriage. It is so important to be aware of these tactics of the enemy so you can be equipped and prepared to overcome!

PRAYER OF ACTIVATION AND DELIVERANCE

> Father, deliver us from every association of the marine kingdom. God, visit us in the night hour. Visit us in our dreams and visions. Help us, Lord, to see truth. Help us to be free from every covenant of the enemy, in Jesus' name.
>
> I repent of any agreement with the marine kingdom, in Jesus' name.
>
> I renounce any covenant, any marriage under the water, any contract made in the marine kingdom.
>
> God, I ask You to bring healing and restoration to any area that has been stolen or attacked by the marine kingdom.

CHAPTER 10

DESTROYING ATTACKS AGAINST YOUR KINGDOM BUSINESS

We're in a time period when God is raising up kingdom entrepreneurs to help facilitate a move of God in this earth that has never been seen before. I believe the next revival in the earth is through the age of information. What do I mean by that? The e-learning business is exploding in growth. In the next three years, it will be a $325 billion industry. Everyday people are becoming millionaires faster than ever with less work and no overhead or capital because of the age of the internet.

Why am I saying this? God has called many of you into the arena of business and entrepreneurship. Whether this is coaching, creating online courses, or even having brick and mortar businesses, a portion of your ministerial calling has to do with being in the marketplace. Not only am I known around the world for spiritual warfare and deliverance, but I am one of the most sought-after in marketplace ministry. The anointing that God placed upon my life is not only to deal with the enemy but also to help raise up people of influence and wealth for the purposes of advancing the kingdom of God.

I have learned through many years of trial and error. I have been a business person myself, training professional athletes and celebrities and owning a gym down the street from the president of the United States. I was able to apply the wisdom that God gave me in this arena. God is raising up people of influence in the business sector who can fund the gospel—those who have proper motives and a heart to see souls won and people's lives transformed. As I began to develop my own digital agency and consulting for kingdom entrepreneurs, I began to see the warfare that satan was bringing at me because of the authority God had granted me in this area.

The Bible says God *"hath pleasure in the prosperity of his servant"* (Psalm 35:27 KJV). God wants you to prosper in your health, finances, and relationships. Prosperity is not limited to only finances. As I began to develop the vision God was calling me to, I began to recognize the type of attacks that most people in the business sector or who carry a tremendous amount of wealth and influence go through. The Bible says, *"For the love of money is a root of all kinds of evil"* (1 Timothy 6:10 NKJV). Money itself is not evil; money is a tool. Just as a pencil or pen or hammer is a tool, it is nothing without the operator. So money must be looked at as a tool that can be used to further the gospel and to increase the kingdom of God.

The Bible also says money is a defense (see Ecclesiastes 7:12). The problem is there is a fine line that those who have wealth in this world have to walk, and that is proper motive. We are rewarded based upon the motives of our heart, whether they be good or bad. When God is raising you up in business, you must consistently press toward Him to purify your motives and to remove anything that is not of Him. As you continually deal with your heart, you will be prepared to handle breakthrough and blessing in this area.

As I began to consult for some of the richest, most influential people in the United States, I began to see a trend in how the enemy targets wealthy individuals. One of the temptations satan offered Jesus was all the kingdoms of the earth if He would bow down and worship him. He approached it from the motive of power and success. We all want to be successful in our life, and there is nothing wrong with being successful. We just have to do it in God's perspective through God's timing and in God's way.

WEALTH IN SCRIPTURE

This is how the Bible describes the wealth of Isaac:

> *And the man waxed great, and went forward,*
> *and grew until he became very great* (Genesis
> 26:13 KJV).

At this point in time, Isaac was in Gerar with the Philistines. There was famine, yet Isaac prospered. The New International Version says, "*The man became rich, and his wealth continued to grow until he became very wealthy.*" The reason for this supernatural growth is found in the preceding verse where it says the Lord blessed him. To *bless* means "to empower and to prosper." This basically means that the Lord empowered Isaac to prosper till he became very wealthy.

Check your motives as to why you're in business. What value you are bringing to the table? Are you running your kingdom business in a way in which God can look at you and bless you? Deuteronomy 8:18 (KJV) says:

> *But thou shalt remember the Lord thy God:*
> *for it is he that giveth thee power to get wealth,*
> *that he may establish his covenant which he*
> *sware unto thy fathers, as it is this day.*

> *The Lord make his face shine upon thee, and*
> *be gracious unto thee* (Numbers 6:25 KJV).

> *And the Lord shall make thee the head, and*
> *not the tail; and thou shalt be above only, and*
> *thou shalt not be beneath; if that thou hearken*
> *unto the commandments of the Lord thy God,*

which I command thee this day, to observe and to do them (Deuteronomy 28:13 KJV).

As for these four children, God gave them knowledge and skill in all learning and wisdom: and Daniel had understanding in all visions and dreams (Daniel 1:17 KJV).

Read the prayer below to destroy every demonic assignment against your life and your business, in the name of Jesus.

PRAYER FOR INCREASE IN BUSINESS

Father, I dedicate all my products to You in the name of Jesus. Father, bless all the efforts and the works of my hands involved in my business. Give me and my team favor with customers, in the name of Jesus. Father, help my workers to understand the needs of my customers, in the name of Jesus. Help my sales teams never to indulge in illegal activity but always to efficiently present our goods and services in the right way, in Jesus' name. Help me to always remain ahead and not behind, in the name of Jesus. Help me to always offer my products in the right way, in the name of Jesus. Father, grant me favor to make profitable sales and increase within our business, in the name of Jesus. Create a demand for our goods and services, in the name of Jesus. Father, open up new opportunities and doors for our goods and services, in Jesus' name. Help me to increase my sales and add new markets daily, in the name of Jesus.

I cancel every evil attack against my products, in the name of Jesus. I break the curse of failure upon my business, in the name of Jesus. I speak that the blood of Jesus cleanses my hands and my products from any defilement. Father, let there be breakthrough for me in all my transactions, in Jesus' name. Let the spirit of favor fall upon me in my business, in the name of Jesus. Father, I ask that You release prosperity on the sales of my products, in the name of Jesus.

Let every demonic hindrance to the sales of my products and services be completely rendered useless, in the name of Jesus. I break every cycle of failure upon my business. Let every darkness that has been prepared against my kingdom business be exposed by the light of God right now, in the name of Jesus. Let my products become a dimension of blessing and a foundation of life for other businesses, in the name of Jesus. Father, give me supernatural breakthrough in everything that I do, in the name of Jesus. Give me supernatural breakthrough in every proposal, in Jesus' name. I come against every spirit of fear, anxiety, and discouragement, in Jesus' name. I shall not be confused, in the name of Jesus.

Father, give me the eyes to foresee market situations, in the name of Jesus. Give me wisdom to walk out of any unfavorable business situation that is presented to me, in Jesus' mighty name. Help me to always identify evil business traps and opportunities that the enemy may throw my way, in Jesus' name. Father, erect safeguards and raise a standard to prevent business failures from coming against me, in the name of Jesus. Lord, help me to be on the lookout for ways to provide a better product and service, in the name of Jesus.

Father, let divine wisdom fall upon all those who are supporting me and selling my products, in Jesus' name. I come against every spirit of conspiracy, treachery, and jealousy, in the name of Jesus. Father, give me favor in the minds of those who will assist me in releasing my products to the world that they shall not suffer from demonic attack, in Jesus' name. Help me to keep my eyes open to see any mistakes or faults that may try to overcome me, in the name of Jesus. Father, guide me and direct me to bring a solution to any problem I have with my business, in the name of Jesus. Forgive me for any wrong decision or action or thought that I have allowed into my business, in the name of Jesus. Let the fire of the Holy Spirit purge my finances from any evil work, in Jesus' name.

Prayers to Destroy Demonic Assignments

Destroying the Power of Sexual Perversion

Do not let the enemy beat you down because of any mistake or immorality that may have happened in your life. God has a purpose. He will call you to a higher place in Him and use you for His glory when you repent and allow the cleansing to take place.

I break myself free from every spirit of sexual perversion, in the name of Jesus. I release myself from every spiritual pollution emanating from my past sins of fornication and sexual immorality, in the name of Jesus. I release myself from every ancestral pollution through iniquity, in Jesus' name. I release myself from every dream pollution and defilement, in the name of Jesus. I command every evil planting of seeds deposited into my life through dreams to come out by fire, in the name of Jesus. Every spirit of sexual perversion working against my life be destroyed by the fire of the Holy Spirit right now, in Jesus' name. Every demon of sexual perversion assigned against my life, I arrest you right now, in Jesus' name.

Father, let the power of sexual perversion oppressing my life die by fire right now, in the name of Jesus. Every iniquity of sexual perversion in my life, I renounce you right now, in Jesus' mighty name. I command every power of sexual perversion to be destroyed right now, in Jesus' name. Let my soul be delivered from the chains of sexual perversion, in Jesus' name. Let every cycle of sexual perversion be broken off my life, in Jesus' name. Let the God who answers by fire arise and answer by fire right now. I claim my complete deliverance from the spirit of sexual perversion and immorality, in the name of Jesus. I renounce the lust of the flesh, the lust of the eyes, and the pride of this life, in Jesus' name. Fire of the Holy Spirit, fall afresh upon me and purge me from all defilement in this area, in Jesus' name.

EVERY ASSIGNMENT AGAINST YOUR PURPOSE IS DESTROYED

Be sober, be vigilant; because your adversary the devil, as a roaring lion, walketh about, seeking whom he may devour (1 Peter 5:8 KJV).

We have to make sure that we do not give the enemy any leeway when it comes to the assignment that God has given us to fulfill on this earth. Persecution will arise because of the work of God in your life. This is normal. Jesus said, *"I have told you these things, so that in me you may have peace. In this world you will have trouble. But take heart! I have overcome the world"* (John 16:33 NIV).

I destroy every power of the enemy trying to arrest my life and purpose, in the name of Jesus. Every assignment against my mind that is trying to derail me from focusing on what God has called me to do, I destroy it by the fire of the Holy Spirit right now, in the name of Jesus. Every cycle of rebellion, I renounce you, in Jesus' name. Every cycle of stubbornness, I renounce you right now, in the name of Jesus. Every cycle of backwardness, I break you off my life, in Jesus' name.

I prophesy that I am moving forward by fire, in Jesus' name. I prophesy that I am in alignment with God's will for my life, in Jesus' name. I prophesy that I shall see the goodness of the Lord in the land of the living, and I shall move forward and nothing shall stop me, in Jesus' name. Every agent of the enemy trying to arrest me in the realm of the spirit, release me now, in Jesus' name. Holy Spirit, help me to see beyond the visible and make the invisible real to me, in Jesus' name. Father, set me on fire for my calling, in the name of Jesus. Father, open my eyes and let me have a revelation of Christ, in the name of Jesus. Oh Lord, deliver me from any lie of the enemy, in Jesus' name. Every chain and padlock hindering my spiritual growth, be destroyed right now, in the name of Jesus. I rebuke every spirit trying to blind me and cause me not to hear, in Jesus' name.

O Lord, deliver me from every lie the enemy tries to plant into my life, in Jesus' name. Let every dream defilement that's trying to shift me off course from my calling be destroyed right now by the fire of the Holy Spirit. I choose to believe the report of the Lord. In the name of Jesus, I bind every power behind any spiritual blindness and deafness. Holy Spirit, by Your fire destroy every satanic garment placed on me in my dreams, in Jesus' name. Every enemy of the gospel in my life be bound right now, in Jesus' name. I release myself from every cloud of darkness, in the name of Jesus. I release myself from every cloud of confusion, in the name of Jesus.

Father, let the doors of prosperity be open unto me, in Jesus' name. Let any household wickedness constructed against my life to stop me from fulfilling my assignment be destroyed, in the name of Jesus. Let any road that would be unprofitable for me be removed, in the name of Jesus. Father, establish me as a holy person unto you, in Jesus' name. Father, let the anointing to excel in my spiritual and physical life fall upon me, in the name of Jesus. I shall not serve my enemies; my enemies shall bow down to Christ within me, in Jesus' name. I reject the anointing of non-achievement in my work, in Jesus' name. I pull out every stronghold that has been positioned against my progress, in the name of Jesus. Every stronghold operating within my mind that is full of doubt and unbelief, I pull you down, in the name of Jesus. I destroy any attack of the enemy, in Jesus' name. Let the root of all my problems be exposed and removed, in Jesus' name. Let every serpent that was released against my life in the realm of the spirit be rendered harmless in every area of my life, in Jesus' name. I declare with my mouth that nothing shall be impossible with me, in the name of Jesus. Oh Lord, let Your favor fall upon me this year, in Jesus' name.

DELIVERANCE FROM ANY EVIL INHERITANCE

Christ hath redeemed us from the curse of the law, being made a curse for us (Galatians 3:13 KJV).

But upon mount Zion shall be deliverance, and there shall be holiness; and the house of Jacob shall possess their possessions (Obadiah 1:17 KJV).

I release myself from inherited evil, in the name of Jesus. Father, pour out Your fire to the foundation of my life and destroy any evil planting that may be there, in the name of Jesus. Let the blood of Jesus flush out my system of every inherited deposit of the enemy. I release myself from the control of any problem transferred into my life from the womb, in Jesus' name. Let the blood of Jesus and the fire of His presence cleanse every organ of my body. I break myself loose from every evil inherited covenant or curse, in the name of Jesus.

Oh Lord, let Your resurrection power come upon my health, in Jesus' name. Oh Lord, let Your resurrection power come upon my life, in the name of Jesus. I bind every spirit of death operating against me, in Jesus' mighty name. I release my body from the cage of every household wickedness, in the name of Jesus. I command every evil planting in my life to come out by fire, in the name of Jesus. Let all negative material circulating in my bloodstream be evacuated, in the name of Jesus. I claim my complete deliverance in Jesus' mighty name. Let every abnormality inside my body receive divine healing, in the name of Jesus. I release myself from every inherited disease, in Jesus' name.

NO MORE FAILURE AT THE EDGE OF BREAKTHROUGH

The enemy's purpose for your life is to experience failure at the point where your success is approaching in order for you not to trust in God. Is this the normal trend for your life? If so, you need divine intervention.

The Lord will perfect that which concerneth me: thy mercy, O Lord, endureth for ever:

forsake not the works of thine own hands
(Psalm 138:8 KJV).

Many people suffer in their life from coming to the edge
of breakthrough only to go right back to the cycle of the wilderness. Maybe you've noticed that anytime you come to the
edge of a breakthrough everything just seems to fall apart.
As you pray these prayers, God is going to help you make it
over the hump.

> Father, release Your angels to remove every
> blocking of my physical, spiritual, and financial breakthrough, in the name of Jesus.
> I come against every spirit manipulating my
> beneficiaries against me, in Jesus' name. Let
> God arise and let all the enemies of my breakthrough be scattered. Father let Your fire melt
> away any stone hindering my blessing, in
> Jesus' name. Let the cloud of darkness overshadowing me and trying to stop me from
> moving forward be removed right now, in the
> name of Jesus. All secrets of the enemy in the
> camp of my life that are still in darkness, let
> them be revealed to me now, in Jesus' name.
> All spirits that are planning to trouble me,
> be bound and exposed right now, in Jesus'
> name. Father, help me not to put any unprofitable load upon myself, in the name of Jesus.
> Father, let every key of goodness that is still
> in the possession of my enemy be returned

unto me, in Jesus' name. All the sweat of my affairs in my life will not be done in vain, in Jesus' name. I prophesy that I am pregnant with good things within me and they shall not be aborted by any demonic power, in the name of Jesus.

DEFEATING EVERY SATANIC NETWORK

God is a man of war. *"He disappointeth the devices of the crafty, so that their hands cannot perform their enterprise"* (Job 5:12 KJV). A satanic network comes in the form of a gathering of evil against people. These associations are activated by the enemy to destroy God's plans and purposes in someone's life. *"What shall we then say to these things? If God be for us, who can be against us?"* (Romans 8:31 KJV).

Let every organized strategy by the host of darkness against my life be rendered useless, in the name of Jesus. I command every demonic spirit transferred into my life be cast out by fire, in the name of Jesus. Let every demonic influence targeting my visions and dreams, ministry, finances, and health be completely destroyed right now, in Jesus' name. Let every demonic trap set up against my life be shattered right now, in Jesus' name. I command all evil activities being done against my calling to receive disgrace and confusion, in Jesus' name. Let the angel of the

Lord pursue me and overtake me right now, in Jesus' name. All partners and demonic associations against my life or family, may you scatter in seven directions right now, in Jesus' name.

Father, let my life, my purpose, and my assignment be too dangerous for the kingdom of darkness, in Jesus' name. Let every seductive spirit assigned against my life be exposed right now, in the name of Jesus. Father, help me to accomplish my divine assignment here on earth, in the name of Jesus. Spirit, I command every organized force of darkness against my life to be scattered by lightning, in the name of Jesus. Every demonic network against my spiritual and physical ambition be put to shame, in Jesus' name. I commend every monitoring device in the realm of the spirit being used against me to be rendered useless right now, in the name of Jesus. Every organization of the enemy against my life, receive destruction right now, in the name of Jesus.

YOU SHALL BE THE HEAD AND NOT THE TAIL

Daniel was preferred above presidents and princes because an excellent spirit was in him and the king thought to set him over the whole land. The Bible says that he was able to function because of this excellent spirit in him.

Let all my adversaries make mistakes that will advance my call, in the name of Jesus. I send confusion to the camp of all evil counselors planning against my progress, in Jesus' name. I commend darkness into the camp of my enemy, in the name of Jesus. I remove my name from every book of failure, in the name of Jesus. Father, give me divine power to accomplish what You have said of me. Give me more wisdom then my competitors, in Jesus' name.

Father, let all the adversaries of my breakthrough be put to shame, in the name of Jesus. I claim the power to overcome and to excel in my life, in the name of Jesus. Let any decision by any panel be favorable unto me in my life. I remove my name from any book that would cause failure to be released against my life. Let the anointing of the overcomer be upon me, in Jesus' name. I receive wisdom, knowledge, and understanding to overcome every situation, in the name of Jesus.

Let every negative word and pronouncement against my success be completely nullified by the blood of Jesus. All my competitors will find my defeat impossible, in Jesus' name. Father, let Your wisdom and power come upon me in a measure that cannot be confronted, in the name of Jesus. I claim supernatural wisdom to answer all questions in a way that will advance my call, in the name of Jesus. I receive the anointing for supernatural breakthrough in these matters, in the name of Jesus.

KNOW GOD'S WILL

God's desire is to make His will known unto you. Over and over again, people ask, "How can I know the will of God?" There are many scriptures that show us how we can pull upon God to know His plans for our life. Psalm 32:8 (NIV) says, *"I will instruct you and teach you in the way you should go; I will counsel you with my loving eye on you."* Proverbs 3:5-6 (KJV) commands us, *"Trust in the Lord with all thine heart; and lean not unto thine own understanding. In all thy ways acknowledge him, and he shall direct thy paths."*

Father to whom no secret is hidden, make known unto me everything that I need to know concerning Your will, in the name of Jesus. Father, remove anyone who could be blocking me from seeing correctly, in the name of Jesus. Father, let any idol that may be present in my life consciously or unconsciously in my heart be removed by the fire of the Holy Spirit. Father, give to me the spirit of revelation and wisdom in the knowledge of You. Father, forgive me for any false motive or thought that has ever been formed in my heart, in the name of Jesus. Father, forgive me for any lie that I have spoken, in Jesus' name. Father, open me up and teach me the deep and secret things of Your kingdom. Reveal unto me the mysteries of Your will for my life, in the name of Jesus.

I come against every spirit of manipulation and deception, in Jesus' name. Father, guide me into knowing Your mind on any particular issue. I come against every alignment of the enemy trying to disrupt my emotions to make wrong decisions, in the name of Jesus. Father, make Your way plain before my face, in Jesus' name. Father, reveal to me the secret things and make known unto me Your choice for my life, in Jesus' name.

PRAYING THROUGH BREAKTHROUGH

Bow down thine ear to me; deliver me speedily: be thou my strong rock, for an house of defence to save me (Psalm 31:2 KJV).

Hear me speedily, O Lord: my spirit faileth: hide not thy face from me, lest I be like unto them that go down into the pit (Psalm 143:7 KJV).

Hide not thy face from me in the day when I am in trouble; incline thine ear unto me: in the day when I call answer me speedily (Psalm 102:2 KJV).

Every power that is boasting against my life, be silenced, in the name of Jesus. Let every good thing that has been eaten up by the enemy be returned unto me, in the name of Jesus. Let every power that is trying to chase away my blessings be bound right now, in Jesus' name. Let every unprofitable mark that has been introduced into my life through my dreams be erased with the blood of Jesus right now.

Oh Lord, empower my prayer life, in the name of Jesus. I reject every spiritual contamination trying to stop my breakthrough, in the name of Jesus. Let every negative plan against my life be rendered useless, in Jesus' mighty name. Father, give me the divine prescription for my problems today, in the name of Jesus. Father, give me power to overcome obstacles to my breakthrough, in Jesus' name. Father, let the Word explode in my spirit to bring me to new places, in the name of Jesus. I bind every spirit of negativity in any area of my life, in Jesus' mighty name. Father, help me to be at the right place at the right time throughout all the days of my life, in Jesus' mighty name. Father, make Your voice of deliverance and blessing clear unto me, in Jesus' name. I trample upon every enemy of my advancement and promotion, in the name of Jesus. I paralyze every evil activity operating against my life, in the name of Jesus. I break every evil collective agreement against my life, in the name of Jesus. Let every evil counselor against me be disgraced, in the name of Jesus.

Oh Lord, enlarge my coast beyond my wildest dreams. Enlarge my territory and let the fire of Your Spirit fall upon any demonic prophets assigned against my life, in the name of Jesus. No dark meeting held against my life or my purpose shall prosper, in the name of Jesus. Let the head of every serpent, scorpion, and power fashioned against my life be broken, in the name of Jesus. Let every marine spirit that's targeting my life be bound, in the name of Jesus. Let every evil trend directing my affairs be reversed, in Jesus' name. Anything that is trying to hinder me from greatness, bow at the name of Jesus. Every imprisoned and buried potential, come forth now, in Jesus' name. I command all unfriendly friends in any area of my life to depart, in the name of Jesus. I pull down the stronghold of evil strangers in every area of my life, in the name of Jesus. Any evil transaction currently affecting my life, be cancelled and revoked in the name of Jesus.

I command all the dark works being done against my life in secret to be exposed and nullified, in the mighty name of Jesus. Let every incantation against my life be cancelled, in Jesus' mighty name. Let every spiritual weakness in my life receive strength, in the name of Jesus. Let every financial failure in my life receive restoration, in the name of Jesus. Let every anti-progress altar fashioned against me in the realm of the spirit be destroyed by the fire of God right now. Let every mark that has been put on me in the realm of the spirit marking me for destruction be erased by the blood of Jesus right now.

Father, give me power to overcome every evil obstacle trying to block my breakthrough, in Jesus' name. Let all the satanic kingdoms working against me fail, in Jesus' name. Let all hidden errors in my life be troubled and return back to their sender, in Jesus' name. I frustrate and destroy every instrument of the enemy fashioned against my life, in the name of Jesus. I disarm every household operation from the enemy against my life, in the name of Jesus. I scatter all the evil counselors and conspirators against my life, in Jesus' mighty name. I take authority over every satanic attack over my life, in Jesus' mighty name. No weapon formed against me shall prosper and every tongue that rises against me in judgment I condemn it right now, in

Jesus' mighty name. I stand against every unprofitable agreement against my life, in the name of Jesus. Let every opposition to my breakthrough be destroyed right now. I paralyze everyone behind the extension and the expansion of my problems—they shall not prosper against me, in Jesus' name.

Let God's angels take back any territory that I have lost by any giant in the realm of the spirit, in Jesus' name. I come against every spirit of heaviness, in the name of Jesus. I come against every spirit of sleep and slumber, in the name of Jesus. I bind every spirit of paralysis, in the name of Jesus. I break every unprofitable agreement that I have made knowingly or unknowingly. I break any curse brought upon me by any past generation. Any power that is trying to unseat me from my promotion, be removed. I revoke every satanic decree upon my life, my family, my finances, my health, and in any area of my life, in Jesus' mighty name. I fire back every demonic arrow targeted at me and my family in Jesus' mighty name. Let every decision that was made against my life by any wickedness be rendered null and void, in Jesus' mighty name. I disband any wicked meeting held in the spirit realm against my life, my breakthrough, and my position, in Jesus' mighty name.

GOD WILL ELEVATE YOU

True promotion does not come from man but from God. *"The Lord maketh poor, and maketh rich: he bringeth low, and lifteth up"* (1 Samuel 2:7 KJV). Promotion comes neither from the east nor from the west nor from the south, but God is the Judge. He puts down one and sets up another.

I thank You, Lord, for using me and enlarging my territory, in the name of Jesus. I reject all backwardness, in Jesus' mighty name. Every cycle that wants me to go backward, I break it off my life right now, in the name of Jesus. Let every agent working against my life be exposed in Jesus' mighty name. Father, give me the power for maximum achievement in my place of influence, in Jesus' mighty name. Father, help me to be a voice of peace, deliverance, and power and solution, in the name of Jesus. Give me divine direction that will propel me to the land of goodness, in the name of Jesus.

Every power assigned against my family or my job to torment me, be paralyzed, in Jesus' mighty name. I command any evil thoughts or records planted in anyone's mind by the enemy against my life to be removed, in Jesus' mighty name. I bind every strongman delegated to hinder my progression, in the name of Jesus. Father, bring honey out of the rock for me this month, in Jesus' name. I neutralize all problems originating from the mistakes of my parents or my past in Jesus' name. Let God arise and let His enemies be scattered. Father, enlarge my territory beyond my water streams, in Jesus' name. I trample upon every enemy of my advancement, in the name of Jesus. Let everything that has been designed in the realm of the spirit to stop breakthrough in my life receive destruction, in Jesus' name. Let every financial failure of my life receive permanent solution, in Jesus' mighty name. Let every architect of my problems be dismantled right now, in the name of Jesus.

Whatever is hindering me from greatness, move right now, in Jesus' name. Every imprisoned and buried potential I command you to come forth and prosper, in the name of Jesus. I break the curse of failure and disgrace and shame in every department of my life, in the name of Jesus. Let the anointing to excel and prosper come upon me, in the name of Jesus. Let every satanic power chasing my blessings be paralyzed right now, in the name of Jesus. I frustrate and disappoint every instrument of the enemy that has been fashioned against my advancement, in the mighty name of Jesus. Let every opposition to my breakthrough be destroyed right now, in Jesus' mighty name.

I render every evil attack against my life and my advancements powerless right now, in Jesus' mighty name.

PRAY THE PSALMS

Arise, Lord, in Your anger and lift Yourself because of the rage of my enemies. Let the wickedness of the wicked come to an end, in Jesus' name. Let them be ashamed and brought to confusion together. Lord, let not my enemies wrongfully rejoice over me, neither let them wink their eye that hate me without a cause, in Jesus' name. Let the angels of the Lord chase and persecute the enemies of my soul. Let them be turned back and brought to confusion, in the name of Jesus. Evil shall slay the wicked and they that hate the righteous shall be desolate, in the name of Jesus. O Lord, fight against him who fights against me; contend against those who contend against me. Let all the eaters of flesh and drinkers of blood stumble and fall, in the name of Jesus.

About Joshua T. Giles

Joshua T. Giles is an apostolic and prophetic visionary, author, entrepreneur, and a business consultant. He is known around the world for spiritual warfare and deliverance while operating in the supernatural. He is also known as one of the top business consultants in the nation for his ability to produce supernatural results through God-given strategies and marketing in the digital world.

Joshua is known as a top celebrity trainer and professional sports specialist. He's worked with some of the biggest names in sports, and his training studio was considered the best on the island of Palm Beach, Florida, down the street from the president of the United States!

When it comes to marketing and business, God has given Joshua extreme wisdom. His clients have seen millions of dollars in returns on their ventures, and he's been able to do this by being a seer and in applying God's wisdom.

Joshua has a passion to see people walk in their destiny and fulfill their purpose!

YOUR
Prophetic
COMMUNITY

Are you passionate about hearing God's voice, walking with Jesus, and experiencing the power of the Holy Spirit?

Destiny Image is a community of believers with a passion for equipping and encouraging you to live the prophetic, supernatural life you were created for!

We offer a fresh helping of practical articles, dynamic podcasts, and powerful videos from respected, Spirit-empowered, Christian leaders to fuel the holy fire within you.

Sign up now to get awesome content delivered to your inbox
destinyimage.com/sign-up

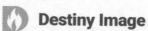